SERIES 3

LEADERS OF OUR TIME

by Robert N. Webb

FRANKLIN WATTS, INC.
575 Lexington Avenue
New York, N.Y. 10022

Cover photo credits:
Brezhnev and Kosygin: *UPI*
Goldberg: *United Nations*
Humphrey: *Office of the Vice-President*
Kennedy: *UPI*
Khan: *Pakistan Mission to the United Nations*
Lindsay: *UPI*
Marshall: *Department of Justice*
McNamara: *U. S. Army*
Pearson: *UPI*
Reuther: *UPI*
Romney: *UPI*

First Printing
Copyright © 1966 by Franklin Watts, Inc.
Library of Congress Catalog Card Number: AC66–10307
Printed in the United States of America

CONTENTS

LEADERS
OF OUR TIME

FOREWORD

A WORLD LEADER may rise to power in many ways, but he must possess ambition and purpose, intelligence, and a willingness to take on great responsibility in whatever job he has chosen. For, no matter what position he holds, a world leader influences the people and the times.

Included among the twelve persons in the third book on *Leaders of Our Time* are heads of government—national, state, and local; leaders in international politics; and those who hold other positions of importance within their own country. Whatever their title, each has made a noteworthy impact on the course of world events in the twentieth century.

The leaders in this book all will leave their names prominently in history. Their actions today may in some way affect the lives of all of us for many years to come.

LEONID ILYICH
BREZHNEV
AND
ALEKSEI
NIKOLAYEVICH
KOSYGIN

THE SOVIET UNION, a nation of one-man rule—in fact if not in theory—since the Bolshevik Revolution of 1917, became a dictatorship without a dictator in 1964. With surprising and dramatic swiftness, Soviet boss Nikita Khrushchev was ousted. Two men—not one—replaced him.

They are Leonid Ilyich Brezhnev and Aleksei Nikolayevich Kosygin. These men divide the power. Both were protégés of the man from whom they seized the power.

Since it is fundamental that a dictatorship demands a dictator, the world has anxiously watched the actions of these two men, waiting to see which one—if either—would take over complete control for himself. The world has also speculated on whether or not another "strong man" was lurking offstage, awaiting the opportune moment to move in and become Russia's dictator.

Neither action took place in the first year of the Soviet Union's two-man rule, nor had it happened when the regime was well into its second year. The political and diplomatic experts who had given the new setup two years at the most now talked less about a single-man takeover.

These experts had every right to question the durability of such a government. For brief periods in the past, Russia had been ruled by a committee-dictatorship. But such actions were only a stopgap while the dictator-to-be got rid of his rivals—in one way or another.

Brezhnev was named First Secretary of the Communist party, and Kosygin became premier of the Soviet. Both positions were held by Khrushchev before he was ousted, as they had been by his predecessor Joseph Stalin, and by Nikolai Lenin before Stalin. To have absolute power, to be dictator of the Union of Soviet Socialist Republics, one man must hold both positions.

Of the two jobs—Party Secretary and Premier—the Party Secretary is considered to be the more important. Although the First Secretary is not a government post, Brezhnev has official control of Communist party machinery. Since there is only one political party in Russia, this gives the first secretary vast powers of patronage. He can select or dismiss Communist party officials, the men who run the country at all levels. He can be likened to the American political boss who stays behind the scenes but controls elections.

Kosygin, as Soviet premier, works as a government official—the top one—and directs Russia's finance, industry, and economic planning. It is Kosygin who deals with the outside world. He is the better known of the two men, since he is more frequently in the news than Brezhnev.

The rise of Brezhnev and Kosygin to the top of Russia's complicated political structure holds certain parallels. Both men are members of the generation which grew to maturity after the revolution. They are the new Russians, sometimes called the Russians "in gray-flannel suits," as opposed to the image of worker Russians. Although the two men came up together, they did so in separate channels. Brezhnev is more the representative of the ideological Marxist Russian, as he must be to guide the destinies of the Communist party. Kosygin is the practical planner, a man of few words who is more concerned with the operation of the government than with party politics.

Both men rose rapidly during the Stalin purges of the mid-1930's, by keeping out of the intraparty power struggles that caused many heads to be lopped off. Both men were in and out of the Presidium (formerly called the Politburo), Russia's permanent governing committee, on several occasions. Both men became protégés of Khrushchev, and both took part in ousting their former leader on October 15, 1964.

After taking control of the government, the two-man collective leadership announced their intention of continuing the posture of peaceful coexistence with the West. Kosygin is known to be more pro-Western than is Brezhnev, an attitude somewhat heartening to the United States and its allies. However, Kosygin did lash out at the United States over its policy and action in Vietnam.

The two leaders were closely watched to see if their actions would bring about any lessening of the split between Russia and Red China. The rift had developed under Khrushchev, but the differences between the two powerful Communist countries showed no improvement in the early months of the new regime. Relations appeared to worsen as the months went by.

Reports of a shake-up in the Kremlin dwindled as Brezhnev and Kosygin settled more firmly into their twin rule.

Leonid Ilyich Brezhnev had been an important, although somewhat obscure Russian official for several years. He became chairman of the Presidium of the Supreme Soviet of the Union of Soviet Socialist Republics on May 7, 1960. As such, he was titular head of state, although the real ruling power rests in the posts of first secretary and premier. A member of the Communist party since 1931, Brezhnev served in various party positions in the Ukraine, Moldavia, and Kazakhstan.

A metallurgical engineer, Brezhnev was a political commissar with the Red Army in World War II. He held the ranks of major general and lieutenant general. Today, he has dismissed his army titles, saying he was a "political general." He was an alternate member of the Presidium of the Central Committee in 1956, and became a full member in 1957. He was a close political ally of Khrushchev.

Brezhnev was born in Dneprodzerzhinsk in the Ukraine on December 16, 1906, the son of a steelworker. He went to work at the age of fifteen, and after work attended classes at a surveying and land-reclamation high school in Kursk where he specialized in farm irrigation. He became a member of the Komsomol, the Communist Youth League, in 1923.

After graduating from high school in 1927, Brezhnev went to work in the Urals for the next three years. He entered the Dneprodzerzhinsk Metallurgical Institute in 1931, getting his engineering degree two years later, after which he worked as an engineer at the Dzerzhinski Iron and Steel Works.

During the Stalin purges of 1936–8, Brezhnev rose rapidly in the ranks of the Communist party of the Ukraine and here he first became associated with Nikita Khrushchev. Brezhnev was head of the Dnepropetrovsk regional committee of the Ukraine Communist party at the outbreak of World War II. In 1943, he was made a colonel of the Eighteenth Red Army, defending Novorossisk. Promotion to major general followed, and he became Political Commissar of the Eighteenth Red Army, a part of the Fourth Ukrainian front.

After the war, Brezhnev returned to party work in the Ukraine. For three years—1947 through 1949—he served under Khrushchev, and his close ties with the dictator were formed during this time. In 1950, Brezhnev was transferred to Moldavia as first secretary of the Moldavian Communist party, and in the same year he was elected a deputy in the Supreme Soviet of the USSR (the Presidium). This was his first post with Russia's national legislative body.

The first check on Brezhnev's fast-rising career came after the death of Stalin in 1953. During the reorganization period, Brezhnev was dropped as deputy premier in the Presidium. Kosygin was dropped at the same time. These turned out, however, to be only minor setbacks for both men.

Brezhnev served next as first deputy head of the Central Political Administration of the Soviet armed forces. He held the rank of lieutenant general and was responsible for supervision of the Red Navy. He was in this position for eleven months.

Brezhnev's interrupted climb up the ladder was resumed in 1954, when he was made second secretary of the Kazakhstan Communist party and was again elected a deputy premier of the USSR Supreme Soviet. He held several other posts in the Kazakhstan Communist party, and his association with Khrushchev was strengthened. Brezhnev directed Khrushchev's plan for the development of virgin land and reclamation of wastelands to increase Russia's grain supply. The success of this operation was a major factor in Khrushchev's becoming dictator of the USSR.

Brezhnev was really on his way now, with no further setbacks. In 1956, he was elected an alternate member (nonvoting) of the Presidium of the party's Central Committee, and became a full voting member one year later. He was named chairman of the Presidium in 1960. In this position, as titular head of Russia, Brezhnev was host to Communist representatives from eighty-one nations, who met in Moscow on the forty-third anniversary of the Bolshevik Revolution. He also traveled extensively, going to North Korea, Morocco, Finland, the Sudan, India, and Yugoslavia. He has never visited a Western country.

Brezhnev was a strong supporter of Khrushchev in Russia's stand against Red China.

The First Secretary of the Communist party is highly regarded at all levels in party circles. His portrait hangs in most Communist homes and in all meeting places.

He is a stocky, bushy-browed man, a dynamic speaker, and is considered a political professional.

Brezhnev has been awarded many decorations, including two Orders of Lenin and two Orders of the Red Star.

Aleksei Nikolayevich Kosygin, the number two man in the Russian political setup, is the Soviet premier. His actual title is Chairman of the Union of Soviet Socialist Republics Council of Ministers.

Kosygin rose through party and government ranks to become one of Stalin's top aides in the 1940's. Serving under Khrushchev, he was recognized as the leading expert on Soviet industry and economic planning. Kosygin is more concerned with practical affairs than with Communist party ideology. He has held many posts since his appointment in 1939 as People's Commissar of the textile industry.

Kosygin was born in St. Petersburg (now Leningrad) on February 20, 1904, of a poor, working-class family. He was thirteen at the time of the Bolshevik Revolution, and at the age of fifteen he joined the Red Army. His enthusiasm for the revolutionary cause attracted attention, and on the completion of his army service he was sent by the government to the Leningrad Cooperative Technical Institute to train as an instructor, organizer, and administrator of cooperatives. In 1924, Kosygin went to Siberia where cooperatives were being developed rapidly. After five years, he returned to Leningrad and entered the Kirov Textile Institute to train as a textile engineer. He had become a member of the Communist party in 1927, having previously been a member of the Komsomol.

Graduating from the Kirov Textile Institute in 1935,

Kosygin became foreman, then shop superintendent of several factories in Leningrad, and later was promoted to the directorship of the October Spinning Mill in Leningrad.

He steered clear of the intraparty struggles that led to Stalin's purges of the mid-1930's, and became one of the dictator's favorites. Under Stalin's sponsorship, Kosygin was marked as one of the rising young Communist officials. In 1938, he was named chairman of the Leningrad City Soviet of Workers Deputies, a position comparable to that of mayor in the United States.

Kosygin first came to a national government post when he was appointed the People's Commissar of Textiles. At the 18th All Union Communist Party Congress in March, 1939, Kosygin made a speech in which he pointed out how far Russia was falling behind other nations in textile production. He was most outspoken, sharply criticizing the policies of other commissars who held positions in the party higher than his own. His words put him on dangerous ground, but he survived. He offered a fifteen-point program, patterned after American production methods, and aimed at getting the textile industry moving.

One year later, in 1940, Kosygin resigned as boss of the textile industry—his program was working—to become deputy chairman of the Council of People's Commissars, and he was made a deputy premier, moving right up to the top level of government officials.

When Germany invaded Russia in the summer of 1941, Kosygin was named a member of the Council of Evacuation in the newly formed State Committee for Defense. With Leningrad under siege, Kosygin displayed his brilliance as an organizer. In one month, January, 1942, he directed the evacuation of 500,000 persons. Then, concentrating on Russia's defense industries, Kosygin, in the early months of the war, greatly increased production in Russia's war-torn factories.

By early 1946, Kosygin had moved up to fifth position among Stalin's eight deputy premiers. He was named an alternate (nonvoting) member of the Politburo, the power center of the Communist party, and two years later was admitted to full, voting membership.

Russia's finances were in bad shape following the war, and Kosygin was the man to whom Stalin turned. Kosygin was made Minister of Finance, and in the unbelievably short period of ten months, he had put Russia's finances on a firm basis, and had turned the job back to the former minister of finance. Kosygin was named Minister of Light Industry, which included the textile industry.

In 1948 and 1949, Stalin was back on the purge path. Many of Kosygin's former associates were cut down. Kosygin survived principally because of his ability as an administrator and planner and because he was not politically aggressive. Stalin did not fear Kosygin.

Kosygin's first setback—a minor one—came at the 19th Party Congress in October, 1952. Stalin shook up his government, replacing the ten-member, four-alternate-member Politburo, forming a Presidium of twenty-five regular members and eleven candidate members. Although Kosygin made a speech highly praising Stalin, he came out of the shake-up only as a candidate member. He continued as deputy chairman of the Council of Ministers and Minister of Light Industry.

When Stalin died, and Georgi M. Malenkov became Russia's premier, Kosygin was dropped from the party

Presidium. He still retained a ministry position, however, heading the newly formed Ministry of Food and Light Industry.

When Khrushchev won out in his power struggle with Malenkov, Kosygin bounced back and was named by Khrushchev as deputy chairman of the Soviet Council of Ministers. He became more closely identified with Khrushchev. He was Khrushchev's chief economic planner, responsible for manpower allocation and raw materials. He set production goals, and fixed prices. He brought about a startling change in Russian industry by instituting incentives for workers and plant managers. In 1960, Khrushchev raised Kosygin to full membership in the Presidium.

Kosygin was elevated by Khrushchev to sole first deputy chairman in July, 1964, a position ranking second only to Khrushchev's. Three months later, Khrushchev was out, and Kosygin replaced his former boss as premier of the Union of Soviet Socialist Republics.

Early in 1966, Premier Kosygin moved into the world spotlight as a mediator when Russia, for the first time, sponsored a move to settle a dispute between non-Communist nations. It was an unusual step for the Soviets to take, and the world followed closely Russia's attempts as a peacemaker.

The disputing nations were India and Pakistan. Premier Kosygin was the host and mediator of the meeting between the late Lal Bahadur Shastri, prime minister of India, and General Mohammad Ayub Khan, president of Pakistan. The meeting took place on Soviet soil in the city of Tashkent.

The big question was the rival nations' claim to Kashmir, as it had been since 1947 when the two independent countries were formed. In 1949, the United Nations brought about a cease-fire, but no further progress was made on the basic question. However, the "Tashkent Declaration," signed by Shastri and Ayub Khan, was considered an important agreement.

India and Pakistan agreed to withdraw their respective armed forces back to positions which they held before the two nations began a three-week war in the fall of 1965. The countries also reaffirmed their obligations to settle their disputes peacefully and to reestablish full diplomatic relations. Prisoners of war were to be repatriated. Right after the "Tashkent Declaration" was signed, Prime Minister Shastri died of a heart attack.

Even though no progress was made toward a definite settlement of the Kashmir dispute, Premier Kosygin did enhance Russia's relations with India and Pakistan, and increased Russia's prestige in all Asia.

First Secretary Brezhnev continued to be the power behind the scenes. There was a shake-up in the Kremlin and in party circles toward the end of 1965. Western experts were not able to read the true significance in the rearrangement of the Soviet hierarchy. Alexander N. Shelepin was removed as a deputy premier. This was interpreted as lessening the power of the man whom many regard as number three in Russia's political leadership. However, a month later, it was Shelepin who went to Hanoi to discuss with Viet Cong leaders the war between North and South Vietnam. It was believed that Shelepin assured the Viet Cong of Russia's support in its effort to drive the United States out of the conflict. Shelepin is regarded as a man to watch as the Soviet moves along under its two-man leadership.

The October 15, 1964, changeover of Russia's government was unlike any changes of the past. There was no violence. Khrushchev was retired and has lived in comfortable quarters with a state-owned car and chauffeur at his disposal. He has not been vilified in the way he himself tore down the image of Stalin, his predecessor.

Western observers interpreted the orderly change in government leadership as an indication that the new generation of Russian politicians was coming of age. Old methods were being replaced. Power struggles involving executions and banishments were not in evidence in the 1964 change of leadership.

But one big question remains in the minds of the experts. Can two heads of state operate more effectively than one? The answer to that question must be delayed until Brezhnev and Kosygin finish writing their chapters in the pages of history.

ARTHUR J. GOLDBERG

"THIS COUNTRY has been good to me. It has given me an opportunity to serve it in the Cabinet and in the Court. These are pretty high honors—there aren't many higher. I have an obligation to this country."

The speaker made that statement at the time he received still another high honor—appointment as the United States Ambassador to the United Nations. He is Arthur J. Goldberg, a man raised in the slums of Chicago's West Side by parents who had emigrated to this country from Russia.

Arthur J. Goldberg has been as good for the United States as it has been good to him. He has served the nation brilliantly in three top jobs—Secretary of Labor, Associate Justice of the Supreme Court, and, presently, as Ambassador to the United Nations.

The former justice was reluctant to accept his new post. But President Lyndon B. Johnson was insistent that Goldberg was the only man who could fill the vacancy left by the death of Ambassador Adlai E. Stevenson in 1965. When the President summoned Mr. and Mrs. Goldberg to the White House to make the appointment, he told them: "When a Southerner can sit in the White House, when a Negro can aspire to the highest offices in the land, when a man of deep Jewish background can be the spokesman of this country to the world—that's what America is about."

Goldberg's short speech of acceptance was moving and eloquent. He said: "I shall not, Mr. President, conceal the pain with which I leave the court after three years of service. It has been the richest and most satisfying period of my career. Throughout my life I have been deeply committed to the rule of law. The law gives form and substance to the spirit of liberty and to mankind's sacred stir for justice. It now comes that the President has asked me to join in the greatest adventure in history—the effort to bring rule of law to govern the relations between sovereign states. It is that or doom—and we all know it. I have accepted—as one simply must."

The United States Ambassador to the United Nations first entered the service of his country in January, 1961. He was the late President Kennedy's selection for the Cabinet office of Secretary of Labor. In making the appointment, President Kennedy declared: "I cannot think of any American who brings greater competence in this field, longer experience, broader knowledge, and a greater devotion to the public interest."

Secretary of Labor Goldberg more than lived up to

the President's high praise for his qualifications. He became one of the most outstanding secretaries in the history of the Labor Department. Goldberg had been in the Cabinet less than two years when another position in the government opened for which he was also eminently qualified. Poor health forced the late Felix Frankfurter to resign from the Supreme Court. President Kennedy acted quickly. He named Goldberg to the nation's highest court. Three years later, Justice Goldberg was again asked to change jobs. He began the third phase of his government service in July, 1965, as the United States Ambassador to the United Nations.

Before entering his government's service, Goldberg had been a highly successful practicing attorney for over thirty years. He is considered one of the nation's outstanding experts in labor-management relations, an ability that should serve him well as he deals with the relations existing between nations.

Arthur Joseph Goldberg was born on Chicago's West Side on August 8, 1908. He was the youngest of the eight children born to Joseph and Rebecca (Perlstein) Goldberg. His parents, poor Jewish residents of Chicago's slums, had emigrated from Russia in the 1890's. Joseph Goldberg supported his family by selling and delivering produce in a horse and wagon. Arthur Goldberg was only three when his father died. When he was twelve, Arthur went to work as a delivery boy for a shoe factory. He went to Benjamin Harrison High School, and by taking extra courses he graduated in 1924 before he was sixteen. He entered Crane Junior College the following year, and in his sophomore year attended Crane and De Pauw University, cramming three years of college into two.

Goldberg switched to Northwestern University. To pay his way and to help support the Goldberg family, he worked nights at the post office, and during summer vacations he worked on construction gangs. He had decided to become a lawyer. Eighteen when he entered Northwestern, he finished the four-year law course in three years. In 1929 he received his Bachelor of Science degree in law and went on to graduate work, obtaining his Doctor of Jurisprudence in 1930, graduating *summa cum laude*. He was the top student in his class and won the Charles B. Elder award. In his last year at Northwestern, he was editor in chief of the *Illinois Law Review*.

Although still not at the legal age of twenty-one, Goldberg was permitted to take the Illinois bar examinations through a special dispensation. He passed them readily and was admitted to the bar in October, 1929. Within eight years he had qualified to appear before the United States Supreme Court.

For the four years following his admittance to the bar, young Goldberg worked for several Chicago law firms. In 1933 he opened his own offices.

Goldberg was an ardent and active supporter of Franklin D. Roosevelt, and through his political associations he met and worked with labor leaders. He first represented labor when he defended the Chicago Newspaper Guild against the Hearst Corporation's *Chicago Herald and Examiner*. It was a long strike, and many of the strikers were arrested on disorderly conduct and contempt charges. Goldberg won a complete victory. None of the strikers went to jail and none of them were fined. The strike ended after nine months, and Goldberg played an important role in the final settlement.

Goldberg had now established a name for himself as a labor lawyer, and soon he was representing other unions, among them the United Steelworkers of America, the United Packinghouse Workers of America, and the Amalgamated Clothing Workers of America.

Early in 1942, following the United States entrance into World War II, Goldberg became head of the Labor Division of the Office of Strategic Services, under its chief, General William J. Donovan. Goldberg performed a most important service in organizing a vast intelligence network of anti-Nazi transportation workers behind enemy lines. He went to Europe on several occasions in connection with this work. He left the service in 1944 with the rank of major and returned to his law practice in Chicago.

Goldberg continued to practice law in Chicago until 1948. At the same time, he became a law professor at the John Marshall Law School and was a lecturer at the Chicago School of Industrial Relations.

In 1948 Goldberg became a national figure in labor-law when Philip Murray, president of the CIO and the United Steelworkers, appointed him as general counsel for both organizations. Murray considered this act the greatest service he had ever made to the CIO. Goldberg was sharply critical of the Taft-Hartley Law and tried many test cases that fell under the law's provisions. His first great triumph was when he won the historic court decision granting that pensions should be considered a legitimate item in collective bargaining.

During this same period, Goldberg was the architect of plans for expelling Communist-dominated unions from the CIO.

When CIO and AFL negotiations on merging seemed to have reached an impasse, it was Goldberg who stepped in and saved the day. As a result of his suggestions, formulas, and compromises, the negotiations, which had broken off, were renewed and the two powerful labor organizations were joined as the AFL–CIO.

The labor movement was under sharp attack for corrupt practices during the 1950's. Goldberg took immediate steps to correct a worsening situation. Under his guidance, an ethical practices committee was formed within the AFL–CIO. Goldberg also wrote the ethical practices code for the committee. Several unions, the International Teamsters among them, were expelled from the AFL–CIO.

During these years Goldberg worked closely with the then-Senator John F. Kennedy in attempting to work out labor-reform legislation. When Senator Kennedy won the Democratic Presidential nomination in 1960, Goldberg became the leader in mobilizing labor to support the Senator.

Goldberg was sworn in as Secretary of Labor on January 21, 1961, by Chief Justice Earl Warren. The next day he was hard at work at his new job, flying to New York City to try to settle the harbor strike which had brought all freight traffic into New York to a near standstill, and which was affecting over one hundred thousand railroad commuters.

A temporary settlement was made immediately, the strikers went back to work, and details for a permanent settlement were worked out a few weeks later.

There was no letup for Goldberg. On the heels of the harbor strike, flight engineers called a wildcat strike against the nation's six leading airlines. Back to New York went Goldberg, and the strike was ended through negotiation.

A major concern of Goldberg's as Secretary of Labor was the high unemployment rate among Negroes. It was twice the rate as for white workers. Goldberg set machinery in motion to combat racial discrimination and urged more Negro college graduates to seek work in the Federal government.

Goldberg held his Cabinet post just under two years, and in that time set one of the highest achievement records of any person holding that office.

The appointment of Goldberg to the United States Supreme Court was highly pleasing to the labor-law expert. It was a job he wanted very much. He felt that the appointment was the realization of a lifelong ambition. Goldberg served only three years as an associate justice of the Supreme Court. But in that time, he wrote over one hundred opinions and voted on more than seventy-five hundred cases. An ardent liberal, Goldberg believed that the Supreme Court should use its fullest powers in the cause of civil rights and civil liberties.

There is no doubt that Goldberg would have been perfectly happy to spend the rest of his days on the Supreme Court. He was quite frank in stating his deep regret at having to leave the Court. "In all candor, I would rather the President had not asked me to undertake this duty. But it appears perhaps that I can, at this stage of our national life, make a contribution. I am very, very sad, but I don't intend to go around mooning about it. I accept—I accept in the full spirit."

In assuming the post of Ambassador to the United Nations, Goldberg took a salary cut from the $39,000 paid annually to an associate justice to the $30,000 paid to the UN ambassador. However, the United Nations job provides Goldberg with an embassy apartment in the Waldorf Towers (annual rental $33,000), a limousine, and a very large expense account.

More importantly, as the United States Ambassador to the UN, Goldberg regained the Cabinet status that he had to give up when he became an associate justice. As President Kennedy's Secretary of Labor, Goldberg's voice was often heard in Cabinet meetings, and not only on labor matters. He gave his opinions on many subjects, and they were carefully listened to. Certainly, in his new position, he will have much to say on America's foreign policy.

The ambassador is of Jewish faith. He stands five feet, nine inches tall; has white, wavy hair; and wears horn-rimmed glasses. His wife is the former Dorothy Kurgans, a painter. They have two children, Barbara Leah and Robert Michael.

Many honors have come to Goldberg. He received the Herbert H. Lehman Medal of the Jewish Theological Seminary, and in 1961 was voted the "outstanding labor personality of the year" by the New York Newspaper Guild.

Goldberg sums up his philosophy of life by quoting the Italian historian Gaetano Salvemini: "We cannot be impartial. We can only be intellectually honest . . . aware of our passions and on guard against them. Impartiality is a dream, and honesty, a duty."

In his new position, the man who has been so successful in his other jobs for the United States is now in a position to devote his talents to the world's largest problem—peace. As a skilled negotiator, as a man dedicated to his country and to the solution of world problems, there is every reason to believe that Ambassador Goldberg will make his presence felt as one of the leaders of the world.

HUBERT HORATIO HUMPHREY

THE OFFICE of Vice-President of the United States has reached major importance, during the last twenty years, in the mind of the American public. Two of the nation's last four Presidents have inherited that position, due to the deaths of the elected holders of the highest office in the land. Harry S. Truman became President on the death of Franklin D. Roosevelt in 1945; Lyndon B. Johnson, after the assassination of John F. Kennedy in 1963.

Hubert Horatio Humphrey is the thirty-eighth Vice-President of the United States, next in the line of succession to the most important, the most demanding job in America—one that automatically thrusts the holder into the role of a world leader as well.

23

There was a time when the candidate for the Vice-Presidency was picked primarily for his geographical location. In other words, if the Presidential candidate was from the East, the Vice-Presidential candidate had to come from the West in order to balance the ticket. His ability to hold the higher office, should that eventuality come about, was not scrutinized as closely as it is today.

The American electorate became keenly conscious of the importance of the number two position in our government during the two terms served by President Dwight D. Eisenhower. Twice President Eisenhower was incapacitated by serious illnesses. During these periods, Vice-President Richard M. Nixon became, in effect, acting President. When President Kennedy was assassinated, a sorrowing nation took comfort in the strength, ability, and experience of his successor, President Johnson. The nation was without a Vice-President during the fourteen months that President Johnson served in filling out the late President's unexpired term. This fact again brought the Vice-Presidency into the sharp light of careful examination.

In recent years, too, the Vice-President has been kept much better informed by the President concerning both domestic and international affairs.

Hubert H. Humphrey, Jr.—he does not use the "Jr." —enjoys a close working relationship with President Johnson. He attends Cabinet meetings and meetings of the National Security Council, and is a member of the National Space Council. He has coordinated civil rights legislation, and is the President's chief link with Congress. Only in the area of foreign affairs is his position somewhat clouded.

Vice-President Humphrey was born in Wallace, South Dakota, on May 27, 1911, and entered the University of Minnesota in the fall of 1929. He was forced to withdraw from the university during the Depression years to help his father run the family drugstore in Huron, South Dakota. He acquired his pharmacy degree from the University of Denver in 1933. Three years later, Humhprey married Muriel Buck. They have three sons and one daughter.

Resuming his education, Humphrey graduated *magna cum laude* with a Bachelor of Arts degree in political science from the University of Minnesota in 1939. In 1940, he earned his master's degree in political science from Louisiana State University. He also taught at both universities. On the United States' entrance into World War II, Humphrey joined the War Production Board and was assistant regional director of the War Manpower Progress Commission.

Humphrey tried again and again to join the Navy, but was rejected because of color blindness.

While a professor at Macalester College in St. Paul, Minnesota, Humphrey decided to enter politics. He ran for mayor of Minneapolis in 1943 but was defeated. He remained in the political arena, however, as state campaign manager for the Roosevelt-Truman ticket of 1944.

Humphrey ran again for mayor of Minneapolis in 1945. This time he was elected, and reelected in 1947. He was a crusading mayor and cleaned up the city, driving out gambling houses and closing brothels. He played a successful and important part in the merger of the state Democratic party and the Farmer-Labor party. One of the first acts in his long struggle for civil rights was the establishment of a council on human relations to investigate racial discrimination problems. He also advocated, and got, the first municipal fair employment practice law in the United States.

Hubert Humphrey's reputation and stature as a politician continued to grow. He was the outspoken champion of the farmer, the laborer, and the small-business man. His round, open, ever-smiling face was known and liked in every hamlet in Minnesota. The letter H for Honesty could well be added to the other three initial letters of his full name. Humphrey built a powerful and highly efficient political machine in Minnesota: its foundation was honesty.

Humphrey ran for senator from Minnesota in 1948. After one hundred days of campaigning and six hundred and ninety-one speeches, he was elected, the first Democratic senator ever elected from that state. It is said of the Vice-President that he can speak on any subject at any time, and he has shown this ability again and again. Once, during his campaigning for the Vice-Presidency, his plane rolled to a stop at an airport at three o'clock in the morning. Surprisingly, quite a crowd had assembled, including the high school band. Sleepy reporters rubbed their eyes as a spruce, smiling, wide-awake Humphrey—he had had only two hours' sleep—came bouncing out of his bedroom in the rear of the plane with the remark, "Boys, I feel a half-hour speech coming on." After speaking twice that long, he hopped into the seven-car motorcade, headed into town, went to bed, and was up at 7 A.M. for another twenty-hour day of travel and speaking.

In his first term as a senator, Humphrey rubbed some of his more conservative Democratic colleagues the wrong way. Even the liberal Democrats were known to frown at him at times. His association with the Americans for Democratic Action (A.D.A.) caused him to be identified as an extreme liberal. He is still a liberal, but no longer considered an extremist. Humphrey was re-elected to the Senate in 1954, and again in 1960. In his learning process, Humphrey had the most outstanding tutor in the Senate, Lyndon Baines Johnson, the majority leader. Humphrey readily admits his indebtedness to President Johnson.

Humphrey became the Senate whip through Johnson's efforts. "I became Whip because he made me Whip. I've had a big, helping hand from Lyndon Johnson ever since I became a member of the Senate." Humphrey's popularity with his fellow senators grew rapidly and his influence expanded. He became a member of the Senate Foreign Relations Committee, and he had an important role in getting Senate approval of the partial nuclear test-ban treaty with the Soviet Union under the late President Kennedy in 1963. His work in the Senate was outstanding. Among his more notable efforts was managing the winning fight in the Senate for passage of the Civil Rights Act of 1964. His opening words on the debate for the passage of the act were: "Until racial justice and freedom are a reality in this land, our union will remain profoundly imperfect. . . . That is why this bill must become law."

The Vice-President has long made civil rights his major concern. At the Democratic convention in 1956, he was instrumental in forcing into the platform a much stronger civil rights plank than that proposed by Truman forces. It was Humphrey's civil rights speech which shot him into national prominence.

Humphrey had his eye on the White House long before he was elected to his present office. At the 1956 Democratic convention, he let it become known that he would like to be Adlai Stevenson's running mate. He campaigned hard for the candidacy. When Stevenson threw the choice open to the convention, and Senator Estes Kefauver was named, Humphrey quickly fell into line and wholeheartedly supported the ticket.

In 1960 he set his sights a notch higher. He announced his candidacy for the Presidency, and ran in the primaries in Wisconsin and West Virginia against the late President John F. Kennedy. Following Humphrey's defeat in West Virginia, he withdrew from the race.

The collapse of his Presidential nomination campaign in 1960 was a serious blow to the ambitious Humphrey. But the resilient Minnesotan refers to it today with good humor. He often tells audiences that he now breakfasts at the White House once a week, adding: "Of course, it's no secret that once, not long ago, I had hopes of having breakfast in the White House *every* morning."

Hubert Humphrey will probably continue to have breakfast in the White House once a week for many years to come. Two factors will control the continuation of this weekly morning meal, the one depending on the other. The first factor is whether President Johnson is reelected in 1968. The second is if President Johnson again selects Humphrey as his running mate. There seems little doubt as to this, since the two men have worked closely together in President Johnson's first term.

Although the man who holds the Vice-Presidency has grown in stature and was picked for his potential leadership, the office itself remains very much the same. The historical restrictions of the position can be most frustrating. Humphrey has all the qualifications for the number one job, but must sit back in the number two position. As Vice-President, Lyndon Johnson experienced the same difficulty. Johnson, an energetic, driving man, long accustomed to power, was almost completely overshadowed by the late President Kennedy. He himself has acknowledged that his years as the Vice-President were "miserable" ones.

President Johnson has done much to see that his Vice-President has a less "miserable" time. Humphrey holds important assignments. He sits in on all meetings and councils at the highest levels. Still, he has less voice in making decisions than do members of the Cabinet.

This is not to say that Humphrey, as Vice-President, has become a man with nothing to do. On the contrary, he seems to be a figure of perpetual motion. The only man in Washington who outdoes the Vice-President in endless, driving activity is Humphrey's boss, the President.

A typical day for the Vice-President starts shortly after daybreak. He quickly reads the morning newspapers while breakfasting. In the Vice-Presidential limousine, on his way to work from his home in Chevy Chase, Maryland, he studies cables, intelligence reports, and top secret material, all aimed at keeping him more up-to-date and better informed than any other Vice-President in history. At his office in the Executive Office Building, directly across the street from the White House, he begins what one of his secretaries calls "another impossible day."

At ten o'clock he is scheduled to address an important

government group. But before setting out for the meeting, he stops at the White House briefly to welcome another group and to give them his views—and those of the White House—on problems concerning the group. His crowded schedule allows him to speak for five minutes. For Humphrey this is clearly ridiculous. Fifty minutes later, having personally shaken hands and spoken to each member of the group—it totaled forty men and women—he is off for his ten o'clock speech, now running one hour behind schedule.

The waiting group, having grown restless, is quickly put back into good humor by Humphrey's opening remarks. He recalls an incident when he was campaigning in 1964 in the northern woods of Minnesota. Then, too, he was late, and his chauffeur was trying to make up time. Humphrey tapped the chauffeur on the shoulder and said, "I'd rather be the Hubert Humphrey who came late than the late Hubert Humphrey."

Following this speech, the Vice-President's original schedule called for him to preside over the opening of the Senate, the one constitutional function of the Vice-President. He makes a point of trying to do this every day that the Senate is in session. But he does not always make it. He doesn't this day. He has to pose for photographs with a new Democratic congressman. Now he has just enough time to be a little late for a luncheon engagement with an important labor leader.

His schedule calls for a two o'clock meeting with Cabinet officers and two hundred mayors who are in Washington to be given detailed information on the poverty program. Humphrey is catching up with himself. He is only twenty minutes late for this meeting. At times, a typical day may continue with a reception, a banquet, and a late evening meeting. It is usually past midnight when he returns to his Chevy Chase home. He must also always be ready for a call to the White House to sit in on any meeting dealing with a new emergency.

In addition to his busy Washington duties, the Vice-President appears frequently in all parts of the nation, attending fund-raising dinners, and addressing meetings of political leaders. Other duties take him out of the country. He accompanied astronauts Edward White and James McDivitt to the Paris Air Show and was the President's representative in England when United Nations Ambassador Adlai Stevenson died there. In early 1966, Humphrey toured a number of foreign nations in connection with United States' policy regarding the war in Vietnam.

Most of these endless activities are assigned to Humphrey by President Johnson. But Humphrey still remains in the shadow of the President. How deep that shadow is depends on President Johnson, who has lightened the shadow as much as possible.

As for Hubert Horatio Humphrey's chances for the Presidential nomination in 1972, many political experts feel that his chief rival may be Robert Francis Kennedy, brother of the late President Kennedy. Although the experts have placed Humphrey ahead of Kennedy in the first years of the Johnson-Humphrey administration, all concede that Senator Kennedy will be a powerful figure at the 1972 convention.

The voters and the changing tides of politics will decide, but Hubert Humphrey's hopes of having breakfast in the White House *every* morning of the week remain high as he continues his duties as the nation's number two man.

ROBERT
FRANCIS
KENNEDY

How FAR, how fast, and in which direction will Bobby run?

The future—like the past—of Robert Francis Kennedy, Democratic Senator from New York, holds many different but related paths.

Since he first entered government service in 1951, Robert Kennedy has been a congressional investigator, a campaign manager, an attorney general, and a senator.

The question concerning his future came into sharper focus on November 22, 1963, when his brother, President John F. Kennedy, was assassinated.

Public and political pundits have kept a sharp, interested eye on the junior Senator. The four goals most frequently speculated upon for Mr. Kennedy in the next six years are: reelection to the United States Senate; governor of the State of New York; Vice-President of the United States; and the top position—President of the United States.

Only Kennedy himself, of course, knows which goal he would prefer. So far, he has not indicated his choice. But from past performances, there can be little doubt that the steely-eyed, square-jawed politician will hit or come exceedingly close to any mark he aims for.

Robert ("Bobby") Francis Kennedy was born in Brookline, Massachusetts, a suburb of Boston, on November 20, 1925. He was seventh of the nine children born to Joseph Patrick and Rose Fitzgerald Kennedy. The Kennedys have always been deeply immersed in politics. Robert Kennedy's grandfathers, sons of Irish immigrants who came to America after Ireland's potato famine in 1847, were both office holders in Massachusetts: Patrick J. Kennedy served in both houses of the Massachusetts legislature, and John F. ("Honey Fitz") Fitzgerald was mayor of Boston.

Animated talk was a family habit. Political discussions —local, national, and international—were always a part of Robert Kennedy's daily life, as they were for his late brother. His father was a dedicated supporter of President Franklin D. Roosevelt in his 1932 campaign. After serving as chairman of the Securities and Exchange Commission, Joseph Kennedy was named United States Ambassador to Great Britain in 1937.

Religion was another major factor in the lives of the Kennedys. Mrs. Kennedy, a devoted Catholic, gave the children a deep sense of religious obligation. The family enjoyed a close spirit of loyalty to one another.

Competition among the children was always encouraged by their father. Although the Kennedys were, and are, a wealthy family, the children were not spoiled by lavish allowances. They were, however, given all opportunities to develop healthy bodies. All were taught swimming, tennis, riding, skiing, and sailing at early ages. Each of the nine children was given a trust fund of one million dollars to be theirs when they reached twenty-one.

One year after Robert's birth, the Kennedy family moved from Massachusetts to a suburb of New York. Much was made of this move when Robert Kennedy ran for the Senate from New York to refute the charge of his being a "carpetbagger" from Massachusetts. Robert Kennedy did spend his childhood in New York, but summered at the Kennedy estate at Hyannis Port on Cape Cod.

Kennedy prepared for college at Milton Academy, Milton, Massachusetts. He entered Harvard in 1943, following in the footsteps of his brothers Joseph and John, and his father. He was in the Navy's V-12 program at college. When his brother Joseph, a navy pilot, was killed on a flight over the English Channel, young Robert left college and officers training to join the Navy as a seaman. He was later commissioned and requested service on the destroyer *Joseph P. Kennedy, Jr.*, named in honor of his brother.

World War II ended before the young Kennedy saw any active service. He returned to Harvard and played end on the football team for two seasons, 1946 and 1947. He was graduated in 1948 with a Bachelor of Arts degree.

Kennedy had decided to become a lawyer and was accepted at the University of Virginia Law School. Between his Harvard graduation and his entrance to law school, he made a trip around the world. In 1950, he married Ethel Skakel, and in 1965 the couple had their ninth child.

He received his Doctor of Laws degree in 1951, and went to Palestine as a correspondent for the *Boston Post*, returning in the fall to take and pass his Massachusetts bar examination.

That same year, Robert Kennedy began his career in public service. He joined the Department of Justice, Criminal Division, and specialized in the prosecution of graft and income tax evasions. His brother John was beginning his rapid rise, and in 1952 Robert Kennedy resigned from the Department of Justice to serve as campaign manager when the late President ran for the Senate. The campaign was successful, due in no small part to Robert Kennedy's relentless drive, organizational skill, and great loyalty to his brother. Kennedy was to prove himself equally successful as a campaign manager when John F. Kennedy ran for President in 1960.

The younger Kennedy returned to government work after his brother's successful senatorial campaign. He became one of fifteen assistant counsels, under Chief Counsel Roy Cohn of the Senate Permanent Subcommittee on Investigations. The late, controversial Senator Joseph R. McCarthy of Wisconsin was chairman of the committee. Kennedy and McCarthy got along well but Kennedy and Cohn clashed frequently. Kennedy resigned when Democratic members of the committee walked out in protest to McCarthy's methods of investigation.

The young lawyer rejoined the Senate subcommittee in 1954 as chief counsel for the Democratic minority.

When the Democrats captured control of the Senate, the committee was reorganized, with the Democratic senator from Arkansas, John L. McClellan, as chairman. Kennedy took a leave of absence from his job for a six-week tour of five Soviet Republics in Asia, accompanying Associate Justice of the Supreme Court William O. Douglas. This tour further broadened Kennedy's knowledge of foreign affairs and enabled him to carry out an important assignment for President Johnson in January, 1964. The President named him as his emissary to attempt to stop an undeclared war between Indonesia and Malaysia. The then Attorney General met with President Achmed Sukarno of Indonesia, President Diosdado Macapagal of the Philippines, and Premier Abdul Rahman of Malaysia. A cease-fire agreement was reached and tension eased somewhat in the Far East.

Kennedy again became a chief counsel in 1955, this time for the Senate Select Committee on Improper Activities in the Labor or Management Field. Senator McClellan was the committee's chairman. The investigation of the International Brotherhood of Teamsters thrust Kennedy into the headlines. The union was then under the presidency of David Beck. When Beck was succeeded by James R. Hoffa, Kennedy began a long battle with the new leader, always giving "top priority" —a phrase he coined—to this struggle. Hoffa publicly accused Kennedy of "wanting to get me personally," but there was no evidence to support this charge. The union was ultimately expelled from the AFL–CIO.

As an investigating attorney, Kennedy was described by Arthur Krock of *The New York Times* as "though very young, he already gives the impression that he is painstaking and accurate," and a *Times* editorial stated, "he asked some very provocative questions." The New York *Herald Tribune* said of him: "His technique as an investigator is to be calm and polite, never baiting a witness. He is not a colorful cross-examiner, but on occasion he can devastate a witness."

When John F. Kennedy was elected the thirty-fifth President of the United States, he named his brother as the Attorney General. There was some criticism simply because the two men were brothers, and it was also said that the younger Kennedy lacked experience for this important post. The President's amusing reply to this charge was that he saw no reason for Bobby's not getting some practical experience before he went out to practice on his own. Lyndon Johnson retained Kennedy in the post when he became President in 1963.

As the Attorney General of the United States, and head of the Department of Justice, Robert Kennedy quickly put to rest the charges that he was too young, too inexperienced for the job. He enhanced his reputation for organization. Shortly after he took office, the entire department was operating at higher speed and with greater efficiency. Kennedy seemed to electrify his people with an *esprit de corps* that had never been equaled before.

Robert Kennedy became a vastly changed man after the tragic November day in Dallas, Texas, when his brother was assassinated. His always slight, wiry body became even slighter. Gray began to fleck his thick, light-brown hair. Deep lines around his eyes became noticeable. Some of the driving, restless energy seemed to go out of his actions. He appeared more introspective, more given to thoughtful deliberation than to dynamic action. Practically all of his adult life had been devoted to serving the late President. He had sacrificed his own ambitions and desires for his brother. It was Bobby who had had to be the hard-driving man who could, and did, say no—while the President was the diplomat.

Robert Kennedy has had to reshape his entire life since the death of his brother. With the passing of time, he has recovered from the shock that overwhelmed him immediately following the assassination. Some of the sharp pain has receded, but his late brother's image is never far from his mind. This was demonstrated when Robert Kennedy first went to Washington as the senator from New York. One of his aides asked him if he wanted the same senatorial assignment that "Jack had had." Kennedy's steel-blue eyes stared back at the speaker. The aide apologized. "I would have said Senator Kennedy, but there are so many of them." The new senator devastated the aide with the parting remark, "You might have said *President* Kennedy."

The speculation as to Robert Kennedy's future has always been a popular subject. Much of that speculation now seems strange indeed, as the political wheels have turned. But it was quite real at the time that the political prophets, and others, stated their long-range views about Robert Kennedy. Six months before President Kennedy's death, there was much serious talk about a Kennedy dynasty in the White House. The buildup for Robert Kennedy to succeed his brother came early in 1963. Gore Vidal, the playwright and longtime friend of President Kennedy, wrote that the political machinery was already being oiled to get Robert Kennedy, then Attorney General, into the White House in 1968.

Writing in *Esquire* magazine in March, 1963, the playwright stated, "Bobby will have the support of the

Kennedy political machine, easily the most effective in the history of the country. . . . Backed by the President and the machine, with an image already floodlit by favorable publicity, one cannot imagine any Democrat seriously opposing Bobby at the '68 Convention. The buildup for '68 has begun. It now follows a familiar pattern."

The author then wrote of Robert Kennedy's civil rights activities, his world travels, his record as an organizer, and as Attorney General.

"There is no doubt that when Bobby goes before the Convention in '68 he will seem beautifully qualified— and from the point of view of sheer experience, he *will* be qualified. But there are flaws in his *person* hard to disguise. For one thing, it will take a public-relations genius to make him appear lovable. He is not. His obvious characteristics are energy, vindictiveness, and a simple-mindedness about human motives which may yet bring him down. To Bobby the world is black or white. Them and us. He has none of his brother's human ease; or charity."

Robert Kennedy maintains those qualities today. He has increased his political stature by being elected the senator from New York. But an assassin's bullets put an end to any plan he might have had for entering the White House as early as 1968.

In 1964, with President Johnson in the White House, the speculation and buildup began as to Robert Kennedy's chances for assuming the number two position, the Vice-Presidency. One comment was: "Robert Kennedy is interested in becoming Vice-President. He never could have run for that office on a ticket headed by his brother. But many party leaders think of him as the logical choice for the number two spot when the Convention meets."

Another comment was: "Mr. Johnson knows that the Attorney General has close ties with political leaders all over the country, ties that can be useful to a President in an election year. Bobby has kept a finger in party affairs right down to the county-chairman level."

There was much speculation, too, at the time, that President Johnson and Robert Kennedy had never been close, going so far as to hint that Kennedy had opposed the selection of President Johnson as his brother's running mate. In any event, President Johnson eliminated Kennedy as a possibility for the Vice-Presidency, as he did all members of his Cabinet. When the Convention met in August, 1964, President Johnson picked Hubert Humphrey, and the Minnesota senator was nominated by acclamation.

Robert Kennedy ended all further talk about his White House possibilities for 1968, when he successfully ran for senator from New York State. As such, he holds a highly responsible position, which could be the first step upward to the highest post in the land. Some think that he will run for governor of New York. The decisive year will be 1970, when Senator Kennedy's present term expires, and when the race for governor will also be run.

There are those who look beyond 1970 to 1972. The question they ask is: Will the battle for the Democratic nomination for President be between Vice-President Humphrey and Robert Francis Kennedy? Senator Kennedy will be forty-seven years old at that time, only four years older than his brother was when he was elected President.

No matter what Robert Kennedy's future holds—senator, governor, or President—he has added his name to the pages of political history. As 1972 approaches, there seems little doubt that Robert Francis Kennedy will figure prominently in the headlines.

MOHAMMAD
AYUB KHAN

PAKISTAN, one of the new nations created since World War II, has existed and thrived despite being surrounded by enemies and being torn by the opposing political ideologies of West and East.

Carved out of the Indian subcontinent in 1947, Pakistan has maintained its uneasy existence under the strong leadership of a man who has developed the skill of diplomatic fence-straddling to a high degree.

He is Mohammad Ayub Khan, president of Pakistan since 1958, a British-trained military man who rules his country with a firm but benevolent hand.

Ayub Khan's government has been called a "naked military dictatorship." It has also been called a "basic democracy," a form of government that could become the model for other new nations in Asia and in Africa.

When Great Britain agreed to surrender its sovereignty over India under the Indian Independence Act of August 15, 1947, the former Indian Empire was divided into two self-governing nations. The division was made along religious lines. The major Muslim areas became Pakistan, its two sections divided by one thousand miles. The Hindu areas remained Indian.

Since that division, India and Pakistan have been in dispute on several occasions. The most serious danger of all-out war came in the fall of 1965, when Indian and Pakistani troops clashed in a three-week conflict.

Compared to India, Pakistan is a small country. Its population is around 95 million while India's population is nearing the 500 million mark. Pakistan's armed forces number around 250,000; India's—850,000. That the smaller country can stand up against the larger is due to the quality of its fighting forces, trained to a high degree of effectiveness by General Mohammad Ayub Khan.

The 1965 conflict between India and Pakistan was over Kashmir, the basis of disagreement between the two nations since 1947. Kashmir, a Himalayan state, has a population of four million. It is 77 per cent Muslim, but is governed by Hindu leaders. In 1947, a Muslim uprising caused Kashmir's ruler, Maharajah Hari Singh, to call for aid from India. He formally conveyed the state to India, increasing the bitterness of Pakistan toward India. The United Nations arranged a cease-fire, and in 1949 Kashmir was split, one third going to Pakistan, two-thirds to India. A plebiscite was to be held to determine the wishes of the Kashmir people, whether they wanted to go with Pakistan or India. The plebiscite, ordered several times, has never been held. Pakistan wants it. India does not—probably because the people might well decide to become a part of Pakistan, since the majority are Muslims.

In 1965, the conflict over Kashmir caused Ayub Khan to exercise his greatest skill in fence-straddling. He has always stated openly his fear of India and his belief that it is India's ultimate aim to take Pakistan back as a part of India. To forestall this possible move, Ayub Khan made a border agreement with Red China. The arrangement caused alarm in the West, particularly in the United States. When the United States cut off aid to Pakistan, relations between the two countries quickly deteriorated.

Since then, relations between Pakistan and the United States have blown hot and cold. In 1954, Pakistan elected to follow a strong pro-American course and became a member of the anti-Communist military alliances in South Asia and in the Middle East.

From 1954 to 1958, Pakistan received $75,000,000 from the United States to use in building up its army. The sum was out of an original commitment of $170,-000,000, the remainder of the money going to the Pakistani air force for jet fighters. Since that time, United States aid to Pakistan has reached nearly $4,000,000,000.

In 1963, the United States supplied arms and equipment to India during its brief border war with Red China. The Pakistani greatly resented the gesture. They felt that the U.S. aid could be used against them as well as against Red China.

By 1965, relations between the United States and Pakistan had reached rock bottom. Ayub Khan visited the United States and entered into discussions with

President Johnson. The talks benefited both nations. President Johnson made it clear to Ayub Khan that American aid to India was intended only to bolster India's strength against Red China and was not aimed at Pakistan. President Ayub Khan, in turn, stated that his recently negotiated ties with Red China were made only to put Pakistan in a better position against India, and were in no way aimed at his nation's relations with the United States. The conference cleared a lot of troubled air, and Pakistan's anti-American feelings decreased.

Mohammad Ayub Khan was born around 1908 in Abbottabad in the northwest section of what was then the Indian Empire. He was the son of a noncommissioned officer (bugler-major) in the British army. A Muslim, Ayub Khan is of Pathan (Indo-Iranian) stock. He attended the Aligarh Moslem University, and then went on to the Royal Military College at Sandhurst, England. He graduated with honors in 1928 and was commissioned and assigned to the Royal Fusiliers. After one year, he was posted to the First Battalion of the Fourteenth Punjab Regiment.

In World War II, Ayub Khan served valiantly with the British army on the Burma front, and during the latter part of the war he was one of the few natives of India to command a battalion. In 1947 he had risen to the rank of colonel.

When Pakistan became a self-governing nation in 1947, the Fourteenth Punjab Regiment became a part of the Pakistan army. Ayub was a brigadier in command of the Pakistan troops at Waziristan, a trouble spot in West Pakistan. He was transferred to East Pakistan in December, 1948, promoted to the rank of major general, and was the first commander of the East Pakistan Division of the army.

By 1950, Ayub had become an adjutant general. He attended training exercises of NATO in West Germany, and during his stay visited England, Austria, and Trieste. In 1951, he was named the first Pakistani commander-in-chief of the army with the rank of full general.

Ayub visited the United States in 1953 for the purpose of inspecting U.S. military installations, and it was during this visit that negotiations were held for United States financial aid to Pakistan.

On his return, General Ayub added an Army School of Education and Military College to the Pakistan Military Academy and Staff College at Quetta. Strict training and modern methods built Pakistan's armed forces up to 250,000 efficient and skilled fighting men.

Internal dissension was eating away at the Pakistani government. Prime Minister Liaquat Ali Khan was assassinated in 1951. Corruption became even more widespread, and friction with India over Kashmir increased. Governor General Ghulam Mohammad declared a state of national emergency, forcing the new prime minister, Mohammad Ali, to accept Iskander Mirza as Minister of the Interior and General Ayub as Minister of Defense as well as commander-in-chief of the armed forces.

By August, 1955, Mirza had become governor-general of Pakistan. Elections were held, a new constitution was drawn, and the country became the Islamic Republic of Pakistan, with Mirza as its president. Pakistan remained a member of the British Commonwealth and continued its membership in the United Nations and the Middle East and Southeast Asia Treaty Organizations.

Trouble continued in Pakistan and, in 1958, President Mirza was forced to abrogate the constitution and declare martial law. He called upon the army to "save the nation."

Ayub moved in quickly, becoming Chief Martial Law Administrator and Supreme Commander of the Pakistan armed forces—army, navy, and air force. On October 27, 1958, Mirza resigned, and Ayub became president by proclamation. When order was restored, Ayub admitted in an interview with *The New York Times* that he had "turned President Iskander Mirza out of office because the armed services and the people demanded a clean break with the past."

Ayub's first public statement was to reaffirm Pakistan's commitments to its treaty alliances. On Kashmir, he said, "We shall be infinitely glad to have settlement through peaceful means. But if forced to adopt measures other than peaceful, the blame will surely lie at the doorstep of India."

Prime Minister Nehru of India replied, "Pakistan is a naked military dictatorship."

General Ayub Khan's sudden rise to the presidency of Pakistan by proclamation did look like the classic military take-over. But the outside world learned that while the general's rule may be authoritarian, it is far different from a severe dictatorship.

President Ayub Khan's "basic democracy" is not a democracy as the word is understood in the West. It is a democracy under the direct guidance of its leader. On

taking office, President Ayub Khan stated, "Our ultimate aim is to restore democracy, but of a kind that
people can understand and work." His "basic" democracy has shifted the elective process down to the lowest
level, the grass roots. The electorate does not vote
directly for national representatives. It elects representatives of its own villages and towns, and these representatives govern. They control the police, supervise the
schools, and collect taxes. The national government
remains in the firm control of the president. He has
eliminated corruption and has strengthened Pakistan's
economy. The nation was on the verge of bankruptcy
when Ayub took over.

There has been much building, and Pakistan's road
system has been greatly enlarged. The illiteracy rate
remains one of the highest in all Asia, but here, too,
progress has been made under Ayub's presidency.

In 1965, a national election was held, and Ayub Khan
became Pakistan's first elected president. His Pakistan
Muslim League party increased its majority in the national legislature from sixty-six to seventy-seven per
cent. He told the people, "My government will be more
in touch with the elected representatives of the people
than ever before." He began a program of setting up
"forums of intellectuals, experts, and knowledgeable
persons." He also informed his people that he would
"welcome a personal letter from any source if it has an
original or workable idea."

President Mohammad Ayub Khan was raised from
full general to the rank of field marshal after his election. He remains every inch the soldier, looking very
British with his clipped, military mustache. He is a big

man, six feet two inches tall, and weighs two hundred and ten pounds. His interests outside of government are widely varied. He is an avid reader, likes gardening, golf, and tennis, and finds time to go "shooting" several times a year. The Sandhurst military training is still very much with President Ayub Khan, as evidenced by his frequent use of the phrase "you chaps" when speaking to a group.

President Ayub Khan must continually direct his attention to many parts of the world. He must keep on a friendly footing with Red China, Russia, and the United States in order to keep Pakistan moving. But most of all, Ayub Khan keeps a close watch on India, the nation he still believes to be the greatest threat to his country's existence.

Early in 1966, tensions were lessened somewhat with the signing of the "Tashkent Declaration" by the late Prime Minister Lal Bahadur Shastri of India and President Ayub Khan. The meeting took place in Tashkent, Russia, with Soviet Premier Aleksei N. Kosygin as host. The declaration covered many points. Among the important ones was the agreement by the two nations to pull back their respective armed forces to positions occupied before the three-week war in the fall of 1965. They further agreed to settle their disputes peacefully and to renew full diplomatic relations.

No final agreement was reached, however, on Kashmir. It still remains under the dual control of India and Pakistan. Until a settlement of the problem, President Ayub Khan feels that he must keep his armed forces on the alert.

While the "Tashkent Declaration" provides for

peaceful settlement of all problems between Pakistan and India, experts feel that the Kashmir problem will not be settled in this fashion. And until that basic disagreement is solved, India and Pakistan will continue to look warily at one another and to keep their military power in readiness.

JOHN V. LINDSAY

THE JOB THAT HE HOLDS has been described as "a graveyard of political ambitions," but the description may well change in the next few years. The post may become the springboard to the highest office in the land —the Presidency of the United States.

The job is that of being mayor of New York City. The man holding it is young, handsome John V. Lindsay. At the time of his election in 1965, he became the first Republican mayor of New York in twenty-five years, and only the third Republican to hold that office since the turn of the century.

Mayor Lindsay has made no public statement saying that he may aspire to change his residence from Gracie Mansion—the mayor's home in New York—to the

White House in Washington. On the contrary, he has ruled out any possibility that he might be a Presidential candidate in 1968. On a television program shortly after his election, and before he was sworn in as New York's one hundred and third mayor, he stated bluntly that he intended to fulfill his four-year term, which ends in 1970. Asked about the possibility of his running for President in 1972, he hedged. He has said though, "It will take eight years to do what has to be done [for New York City]. If my record is good after one term, I would hope I could get reelected. I want to be a good mayor."

If he does establish a record as a good mayor and makes notable headway in solving the many and gigantic problems besetting the nation's largest city, John V. Lindsay will no doubt become the outstanding man for the Republican nomination for President in 1972.

As this nation becomes more and more urbanized, men who can handle the staggering problems accompanying this urbanization will become standouts. In the past, the governorships and the Senate have often been the cradles of the Presidency. In the future, the cities may become the stages where political spotlights pick out Presidential candidates.

New York City is considered the most problem-ridden of all the country's cities. In campaigning for the office of mayor, John Lindsay said over and over again, "Let us make our city great again, the Empire City of the World." Accomplishing this will indeed be a giant step toward the White House.

It will be a most difficult step, however, for the job of mayor of New York has also been described as "one of the toughest in the world."

Lindsay found this out on January 1, 1966, the day he was sworn in as mayor. A transit strike was called, crippling the city for thirteen days. Working day and night to settle the strike, Lindsay had to put aside his plans for solving New York's other problems. The mayor walked to work on many days, striding briskly along the four miles to his office at City Hall. Constantly appearing on television and speaking on radio to inform the public of developments, Lindsay became well known to the people of New York in a very short time.

Some of the problems which faced Mayor Lindsay on his take-over included: a rapidly rising crime rate—a murder a day, a theft every three minutes, and an assault every twelve minutes; an incredibly snarled traffic situation; air pollution—two tons of soot fall on every square mile of Manhattan Island daily. As if that was not enough, the city was deep in debt. Interest on the debt alone was 1.4 million dollars daily. The city's slum areas are near total decay, requiring new housing units to care for one million tenement dwellers. New York City has largely been abandoned by one million middle-income-group whites, who are being replaced by Negroes and Puerto Ricans at the bottom of the income groups.

It has been said that only the very rich or the very poor can afford to live in New York City.

Lindsay's task in solving the city's problems is further complicated by the fact that he is a Republican surrounded by officials who are predominantly Democratic. He won the election by more than 125,000 votes over his closest opponent. With this somewhat slim margin (out of a total of more than 2.5 million votes cast), he was not able to carry his ticket into office with

him. The two other top officials at City Hall are Democrats. Of the thirty-seven City Councilmen, thirty are
Democrats. They have the power to put through Democratic measures not necessarily in line with Mayor
Lindsay's aims. As for fiscal measures, these are handled
by the Board of Estimate. Of its twenty-two votes,
only a small minority were counted as being in Mayor
Lindsay's camp when he took over.

Yet John Lindsay was surrounded by opposition
when he ran for mayor, and he came out on top. New
York City is predominantly Democratic—of its more
than 7.5 million residents, the registration of Democratic voters over Republicans is seven to two. In running for mayor, Lindsay played down his Republican
label. He did not deny his being a Republican. However, he said, "I am a Republican, but New York City
must have an independent, nonpartisan government."

He ran "as Lindsay." He pointedly asked Republican VIP's to stay out of New York during his campaign. These VIP's included New York's Governor
Nelson A. Rockefeller and former Vice-President
Richard Nixon, now a New York City resident.

"I don't need officialdom to build me up," Lindsay
said. "I don't think the public will vote for me just because a distinguished person says they should."

Lindsay did not increase his popularity rating among
the leaders of the Republican party by this action. In
fact, he alienated many. But his strategy proved correct.
Lindsay's percentage of the city-wide vote in New
York was almost double that polled by the Republican
Presidential candidate Barry Goldwater in 1964 for the
same area.

Goldwater was one Republican who was not jubilant

about Lindsay's victory. "Lindsay," he commented, "feels that anything that can be done to win an election should be done, even if it means completely forgetting Republican principles."

Quick to dispute this view was the Republican party's National Chairman Ray Bliss. He disagreed with the opinion that Lindsay's independent campaign downgraded the victory as a Republican one. "He ran on the Republican ticket," Bliss pointed out. "He's a Republican and everybody knows he's a Republican."

Former Vice-President Richard Nixon disagreed. "It is a Lindsay rather than a Republican victory. Had he run as an old-line Republican regular, he wouldn't be mayor today."

Jubilant Republican moderates could not agree more with Nixon. To them, Lindsay's victory is a big step in rebuilding the Republican party. They see him as the one best hope for bringing the party back from its disastrous defeat in 1964.

Since he ran for mayor "as Lindsay," his victory did bring up the question as to what kind of a Republican he is. Some party members claim that he is a poor Republican. Others say that he is anything but a Republican. But an increasing number of Republicans, and many independent voters, look toward John Lindsay as the one man today who may become the party's best hope for again winning national office.

In January, 1959, John Lindsay entered Congress from New York's 17th Congressional District, called the "Silk Stocking" district because it includes wealthy residential sections of the city. From the start he showed himself to be "a loner." He disregarded the unwritten law of Congress that a freshman member should remain silent during his first session—that "to get along," he must "go along." Lindsay, in his first month as a congressman, was in sharp disagreement with a fellow member of Congress, very much his senior. In fact, this member had twenty-five years' seniority over the freshman from New York. The elder congressman had delivered a stinging attack on the Supreme Court, charging that the Court, under Chief Justice Earl Warren, was doing away with precedents and substituting "Socialist doctrines."

Lindsay was unable to remain silent. He rose to his feet, and after paying his respect for "the remarks of my distinguished senior," he went on to say "I am constrained to disagree with him." He stated that historians would label the Warren Court as "one of the great courts of our country." He went on to defend President Eisenhower's appointment of Warren, as the Chief Justice, as meeting "the highest standards of the legal profession."

Lindsay's voting record in Congress gives some indication of the kind of Republican that he is. The record shows that his votes were more liberal than those of many Democrats. During Lindsay's first two terms as a congressman he voted with the majority of Republicans three times out of five. In his third term (1963–4) he voted only one out of three times with the Republican majority. President Eisenhower was still in the White House during Lindsay's first term. Lindsay supported the President four times out of five, an average above the overall support by Republican members of Congress. Lindsay's support of Presidential measures continued during the Kennedy Administration. During the first two years, he cast his vote in support of key issues

Hubert H. Humphrey, thirty-eighth Vice President of the United States (*Office of the Vice President*)

Arthur J. Goldberg, permanent representative of the United States to the United Nations, holds a press conference. (*United Nations photo*)

Secretary of Defense Robert S. McNamara (*U.S. Army photograph*)

John V. Lindsay receives a carnation as he is "off and running" in a successful bid for mayor of New York City. (*UPI photo*)

Senator Robert F. Kennedy arrives in New York City. (*UPI photo*)

Above: Canada's Prime Minister Lester B. Pearson stands between two members of his cabinet. (*UPI photo*)

Left: A smiling Walter Reuther, head of the United Automobile Workers, faces the press. (*UPI photo*)

Above: Michigan Governor and Mrs. George Romney meet with Republican Wayne Dumont, who unsuccessfully ran for governor of New Jersey in 1965. (*UPI photo*)

Right: Solicitor General Thurgood Marshall (*Department of Justice*)

Left: The president of Pakistan, Mohammad Ayub Khan (*Pakistan Mission to the United Nations*) Right: Premier Aleksei Kosygin of the Soviet Union at a press conference (*UPI photo*)

U Thant, Secretary-General of the United Nations, visits the Soviet Union's First Secretary of the Communist party, Leonid Brezhnev (third from right) in Moscow. (*UPI photo*)

two out of three times. This was stepped up to three out of four during the next two years with President Johnson in the White House. In all, without regard to whether a Republican or a Democrat occupied the White House, Lindsay's support of Presidential measures was much higher than the overall support by Republican members.

Lindsay's attendance record in Congress was remarkable. During the last session of the Eighty-sixth Congress (1960) he missed only one vote. The occasion was the birth of his fourth child, Johnny. His frequency of voting record stands at 98 per cent in his first term, 94 per cent in his second, and 89 per cent in his third term—a record considerably higher than that of the average congressman.

John Vliet Lindsay and his twin brother David were born November 24, 1921, in an unpretentious apartment on the West Side of Manhattan. As his father's fortunes improved, so did the family addresses. George Nelson Lindsay, John's father, was the son of a Scottish-Irish brickmaker from the Isle of Wight. He went broke in 1884 and emigrated to New York. He was a self-made man, rising to become vice-president of a Wall Street investment house. He died in 1962, leaving a fortune of $700,000. The money was divided among John, David, George, and Robert. (The daughter of the family, Eleanor, drowned in her swimming pool in the summer of 1965.)

John's mother, a graduate of Wellesley College, had aspirations for the stage until she met George Lindsay. She gave up her dreams of the stage to settle down with her husband, who was on his way up the Wall Street ladder.

John Lindsay attended the exclusive Buckley School in Manhattan for his elementary education, then went on to the equally exclusive St. Paul's school in Concord, New Hampshire. At St. Paul's, he played center on the football team, was a member of the crew, a member of the debating team, and president of his class. He graduated in 1940 and entered Yale University. With World War II drawing near, John took the accelerated course at Yale, getting his Bachelor of Arts degree in thirty-one months. His undergraduate thesis was on "The Effect of Oliver Cromwell's Religion on Politics."

After graduation, Lindsay entered the Navy with an ensign's commission. The next three years he served aboard the destroyer *Swanson*. As a gunnery officer, he saw action in the Mediterranean, taking part in the invasion of Sicily. During this action, his ship was rammed by another destroyer and nearly sank. After nine months of service in the Mediterranean and the Atlantic, the *Swanson* sailed for the Pacific. There, for two years, Lindsay served in the 7th Amphibious Fleet in the Southwest Pacific. The destroyer took part in landings on Biak, Hollandia, and the Admiralty Islands, then joined the 5th Carrier Strike Fleet for the invasion of the Philippine Islands.

At the war's end, Lindsay had earned five battle stars, was a full lieutenant, and had become his ship's executive officer.

In the fall of 1946, Lindsay entered Yale law school and again cut short the ordinary time required to win a law degree. He finished the three-year course in two years, receiving his degree in 1948.

While attending law school, Lindsay met Mary Anne Harrison, a Vassar girl from Greenwich, Connecticut.

She matched her future husband's pace, finishing Vassar in three years instead of the customary four. She taught school, first in Providence, Rhode Island, then at the same Buckley School that John had attended. They were married in June, 1949, and took a small apartment in Stuyvesant Town, a large development on New York's East Side. The development later became a part of the 17th Congressional District. For a time, Mrs. Lindsay taught in the community nursery school, then gave up teaching to have children of her own. In 1965, there were four young Lindsays: Katherine, fourteen; Margaret, twelve; Anne, nine; and John, five.

In the middle 1960's, as Lindsay's political star began to shine brightly, there were inevitable comparisons of young Lindsay with John F. Kennedy. There were the Kennedy brothers and the Lindsay brothers. But only John, of the Lindsays, chose politics while all of the Kennedy boys had entered the field. The Lindsay fortune cannot be compared to the massive Kennedy wealth, nor was Lindsay's father ever dedicated to making any of his sons a leading national office holder, as Joseph Kennedy had been.

Voters, however, noted similarities. Both J.F.K. and J.V.L. brought to politics the charm and attraction of youth, and young people flocked to their banners. Both Kennedy and Lindsay had backgrounds of Ivy League preparatory schools and colleges. (Kennedy went to Choate and Harvard.) Both were sailing enthusiasts. Both had served in the Navy. As Kennedy inspired youth and gave the promise of new and idealistic approaches to politics, so did Lindsay. Kennedy had an intellectual appeal for voters, and so does John Lindsay.

But to carry the comparison any further would not

be fair. Certainly Lindsay cannot be called "a new Kennedy," nor even a "Republican Kennedy." He is Lindsay, who runs "as Lindsay," but has most definitely been a Republican all of his life.

It is true that he has supported many Democratic-sponsored bills in the House of Representatives. One notable occasion was in 1963 when he supported the Kennedy Administration's bill to cut down the power of the House Rules Committee by enlarging its membership. This stand was personally costly to Lindsay. He had long wanted to become a member of the House Foreign Affairs Committee. His 1963 vote in support of the Kennedy legislation cost him this appointment. The minority whip, Republican Representative Leslie Arends, said to Lindsay: "Boy, I never saw a man talk himself off the Foreign Affairs Committee so fast in my life." Typically, Lindsay was standing firmly on what he believed to be right, regardless of what his fellow Republicans thought.

One of Lindsay's assignments in Congress was to the Judiciary Committee. His record was outstanding. He was one of the drafters of the 1964 civil rights bill and, as one of the floor managers of the bill, was one of its foremost spokesmen for passage in the House. He also was a leader in getting approval of the 1965 voting rights bill.

Lindsay's record as a vote-getter is as impressive as his record as a congressman. In 1960, running for his second term, Lindsay captured 59.8 per cent of the votes in his district. In 1962, he upped this margin to 68.7 per cent of the total vote. His biggest margin of victory came in 1964, the year that Lyndon B. Johnson piled up a tremendous popular vote which swept nearly all Democrats in New York into office on the Presidential coattails. Lindsay was the notable exception. He came through with 71.5 per cent of his district's votes, the largest margin of victory by any GOP congressman in the United States.

John Lindsay sums up his political philosophy in the following words:

"Freedom and politics are inseparable. The quality of our government depends upon the quality of political endeavor. Yet it is fashionable to demean people who run for office, and this discourages good people from political careers. Those who dare to enter find that the most dangerous enemy of government and freedom is apathy. When apathy reigns, the democratic process becomes infected, sickens and dies.

"A government for people must depend for its success on the interest of the people themselves. The way to check the natural arbitrariness of government is to keep government close to the people; and the only way to achieve this is for the people to stay close to government. This means getting involved in the political life of your community and your country. In the final analysis, the best of all government is that which inspires us to govern ourselves. We fail to do so, to quote Justice Oliver Wendell Holmes, only 'at the peril of being judged not to have lived.' "

John V. Lindsay has been deeply involved with the government of his community and his nation for many years. There is a growing number of people in the United States who feel certain that this involvement will become even deeper in the years to come.

THURGOOD MARSHALL

THURGOOD MARSHALL, the first Negro Solicitor General of the United States, may also become the first Negro Justice of the United States Supreme Court. Ever since his appointment to the prestige post of solicitor general, Washington experts have openly predicted that Judge Marshall's present job is only a stopover on the way to the bench of the highest court in the land.

President Johnson, these experts point out, has shown his desire to place qualified Negroes in all levels of government service. He would, they continue, also like to be the first President to appoint a Negro to the Supreme Court.

To become solicitor general, Marshall gave up a lifetime position as a judge of the United States Second Circuit Court of Appeals. This judgeship pays an annual salary of $33,000. As solicitor general, Judge Marshall will earn $4,500 less per year, and the post is not secure. The Solicitor General is a part of the Attorney General's office, and the post is thus appointive, its duration depending on the man in the White House.

But whether Judge Marshall appears before the Supreme Court as solicitor general, or sits with it as an associate justice, the Court will be a familiar place for him. As Special Counsel for the National Association for the Advancement of Colored People (NAACP), Marshall has argued thirty-two cases before the Supreme Court and won twenty-nine of them.

The most notable of these was *Brown v. Topeka Board of Education of Topeka*, the school desegregation case. It was this case that brought about the Supreme Court's historic decision of May 17, 1954, that racial segregation in public schools was in violation of the Constitution. The Court's decision was unanimous.

This case also propelled Marshall into national prominence and earned him the reputation of being America's outstanding civil rights lawyer. It was a reputation that he enhanced by further noteworthy victories in the field of civil rights.

Other cases that Marshall successfully argued freed Negroes from Jim Crow restrictions when traveling from one state to another; gave Negroes the right to vote in primaries in the South; eliminated restrictive covenants preventing Negroes from buying or renting real estate; and won several cases which involved the exclusion of Negroes from jury duty.

There are few living individuals who have played as important a role in changing the structure of America's social life as has Judge Marshall.

Thurgood Marshall was born July 2, 1908, in Baltimore, Maryland. His father, William Canfield Marshall, was a steward at the exclusive Gibson Island Club on Chesapeake Bay. His mother, Norma (Williams) Marshall, was a schoolteacher in a segregated primary school in Baltimore. Marshall's parents were strong anti-segregationists. Marshall's great-grandfather had been brought as a slave to this country from the Congo by a wealthy, big-game hunter.

Marshall tells a story about his great-grandfather, a story which may well give some indication as to where the judge's ability to argue originated. The great-grandfather argued with his master continually on any and all subjects, but was particularly forceful on the subject of slavery. He spread his objections to slavery throughout the countryside. One day the master called the argumentative slave in and said to him: "Look, I brought you here so I guess I can't very well shoot you—as you deserve. On the other hand, I can't, with a clear conscience, sell anyone as vicious as you to another slave-holder. So, I'm going to set you free—on one condition. Get out of this country and never come back."

Marshall grins as he concludes the story. "That is the only time Massuh didn't get an argument from the old boy."

Like his great-grandfather, Marshall has been arguing all of his life. This heritage for debate was also passed on to Marshall by his father. Marshall credits his father with turning him into a lawyer. "He did it by teaching me to argue," Marshall says. "By challenging my logic on every point, by making me prove every statement. He never told me to become a lawyer, but he turned me into one."

Neighbors of the Marshalls, when the family lived on Druid Hill Avenue in Baltimore, could vouch for the argumentative streak that runs through the family. Hardly a night went by but the sound of voices raised high in dispute could be heard coming from the Marshall home. "The lady next door," Marshall recalls, "could always tell when my brother Aubrey and I got home from college." At those times, the arguments became even louder.

Marshall's formal education began in segregated schools in Baltimore. He graduated with honors from Douglas High School and went on to Lincoln University in Oxford, Pennsylvania. He had to work to get enough money to pay for his education. He held many jobs—grocery clerk, banker, and dining car waiter— during his summer vacations from college. His memories of the time spent as a dining car waiter are still close to Marshall. On train trips, during his time as special counsel for NAACP, he was often found in the diner between meals, laughing and joking with the waiters. He traveled some fifty thousand miles a year during this period.

In 1930, Marshall graduated *cum laude* from Lincoln University with a Bachelor of Arts degree. He went on to Howard University in Washington, D.C., with money saved from other jobs, plus money from his mother who had pawned her engagement and wedding rings so that her son could receive his law degree.

Three years later, Marshall was awarded his Bachelor of Laws degree, *magna cum laude*, graduating number one in his class. About Howard, Marshall says, "For the first time I found out my rights." He was admitted to the Maryland bar the year of his graduation, 1933.

Marshall began his law practice in Baltimore. He specialized in civil rights cases and soon built up the largest single practice of any lawyer in the city. Although his practice was large, his income from it was small. Quite regularly he had to scrape pennies together to pay his rent, and it was not unusual for him to borrow lunch money from his secretary. "Word got around," he says, "that I was a 'free' lawyer—that does you no good."

But even if it was "free" work, Marshall threw himself into it with all the vigor and energy that has marked his entire career. Victories in the civil rights cases that he argued were few in those days. But one of his victories was a major one. Prophetically it had to do with school segregation. It came in 1935 when Marshall was successful in getting a Negro, Donald Murray, admitted to the previously segregated University of Maryland law school. This was the first significant "breakthrough" in educational segregation. It was also one of the last cases that Marshall argued as a private attorney.

Shortly after the Murray case, Marshall became assistant to the late Charles Hamilton Houston, who was special counsel to the NAACP. The association was a reunion of teacher and pupil. Houston, considered a most gifted and polished advocate, became head of the law school at Howard in 1929. His goal was to make the law school the cradle of the civil rights drive for the American Negro. To do this, Howard's law school had to be strengthened. Houston scoured the country for the most able instructors and made the law courses extremely difficult. From the student body, Houston selected only the brightest for the special training necessary for the civil rights struggle. One of these students was Thurgood Marshall.

That Houston had chosen wisely was proven when Marshall directed the preparation of the brief and argued the case that brought about the Supreme Court's May 17, 1954, decision, declaring racial segregation in public schools unconstitutional. Additional evidence is found in a statement by Federal Judge William H. Hastie of the U.S. Third Circuit Court of Appeals in Philadelphia. "Certainly no lawyer, and practically no member of the bench, has Thurgood Marshall's grasp of the doctrine of the law as it affects civil rights."

Marshall is not the academic or scholarly type lawyer that his background and impressive list of court victories suggest. He is an informal man, an extrovert, given to witty remarks, loud—even boisterous—joking, able to adapt himself to any environment or the degree of seriousness of any moment. It has been said of him that he "is as comfortable at Hogwash Junction as he is in the home of the Supreme Court. He relates to everybody and anybody and it's this more than anything else that sets him apart from the rest."

He demonstrated this opinion of him in his argument before the Supreme Court in the historic segregation case. He did not go in for stiff language and dry, legal technicalities. He spoke in simple words that expressed his own feelings about racial segregation. Addressing the Court he said:

"Those same kids in Virginia and South Carolina— and I have seen them do it—they play in the streets together, they play on their farms together, they go down the road together, they separate to go to school, they come out of school and play ball together. They have to be separated in school. . .

"It can't be because of slavery in the past because

there are very few groups in this country that haven't had slavery some place back in the history of their groups. It can't be color because there are Negroes as white as drifted snow, with blue eyes, and they are just as segregated as the colored men.

"The only thing it can be is an inherent determination that the people who were formerly in slavery, regardless of anything else, shall be kept as near that stage as is possible, and now is the time, we submit, that this court should make it clear that that is not what our Constitution stands for."

Marshall's ability to adapt to environment becomes evident when he goes south of the Mason-Dixon Line. Before the Supreme Court, he has no trace of a Southern accent. But the farther south he travels, the broader becomes his accent.

In the past, Marshall has gone into the Deep South on many occasions to fight for Negro civil rights. He knows that he faces bodily danger on these trips. In 1946 he went south to defend some Negroes accused of attempted murder during a riot. The case was tried in Columbia, Tennessee. The atmosphere was extremely hostile, so much so that Marshall and his associate lawyers from the NAACP stayed in Nashville, Tennessee, during the trial, commuting daily the forty miles between the two cities.

The trial ended successfully for Marshall. He was driving back to Nashville with two associates when two police cars forced him off the road. The police demanded Marshall's driving license. He produced it and was permitted to continue. A few miles farther on, the same police cars again forced Marshall to pull up. He was accused of drunken driving and having liquor in his car. Marshall got out and watched carefully as police searched the car. He knew of the trick sometimes used by prejudiced policemen of putting a bottle of whiskey in a car while supposedly only searching it. Nothing was found and once again Marshall was allowed to go on his way. Not for long though. While passing through a small town a few miles farther along, the police stopped Marshall's car for the third time. This time they arrested him for drunkenness. Marshall got out of the car. The police officers ordered him and his two associates to cross the street to the courthouse—the police officers would follow. Marshall shook his head. Too often, he knew, Negroes had been shot in the back for supposedly resisting or trying to escape. He insisted that the police officers escort him and his companions by walking side by side.

In the courthouse, Marshall appeared before the local magistrate. He leaned forward and placed his hands on the judge's shoulders and breathed as hard as he could into the judge's face. That ended the case. Obviously, Marshall had not had anything to drink. On finally reaching Nashville he said, "Boy, I really *wanted* a drink."

Marshall has faced much opposition in the South. But from Southern lawyers, he has had high praise. Joseph Greenhill, who opposed Marshall in a segregation case in Texas, said of him, "He was an excellent lawyer in the courtroom. He was courteous, he didn't rant or rave, and he asked good questions."

Another Southern lawyer, Robert Fiff, who opposed Marshall in a South Carolina school case, said, "He is an able lawyer and a skillful advocate. His appeals gain power from his dedication to the cause he presents."

Still another Southern lawyer, Taggard Whipple, who was Marshall's opponent in the historic 1954 Supreme Court case, said, "He was eminently fair. Certainly he is one of the top civil liberties lawyers in the country."

In 1955, after the death of his first wife, Marshall married Cecelia S. Suyat. He has two sons.

In 1961, Marshall was named to the U.S. Second Court of Appeals, which covers New York, Connecticut, and Vermont. Twelve months passed before the Senate confirmed the appointment. During his nearly four years on the court, Marshall wrote more than one hundred opinions. None of these has been reversed by the Supreme Court.

In his new post of Solicitor General, Marshall ranks third in the hierarchy of the Attorney General's office, preceded only by the Attorney General and the Assistant Attorney General. In this post, Marshall's job is to argue the United States government's side in cases before the Supreme Court. He also decides which cases the government should take before the Court.

No longer will he be the leading fighter for the American Negro's civil rights. But certainly he is the man who has done the most in behalf of civil rights in the last twenty years. He closely followed his doctrine that "it is only by lawsuits and legislation that we will ever teach reactionaries the meaning of the 14th Amendment."

ROBERT S. McNAMARA

THE JOB is one of the biggest in the world. The man in charge spends 50 billion dollars yearly. In addition, he oversees more than 150 billion dollars' worth of ships, tanks, aircraft, missiles, and real estate. He is also the boss of four million men and women.

The man on whose shoulders this staggering burden rests is Robert Strange McNamara, Secretary of Defense of the United States, in the Cabinet of President Lyndon B. Johnson.

Spending all that money, managing all that military hardware and property, supervising all those people is just one part of Secretary McNamara's job. He is President Johnson's principal adviser on matters of national defense; he is a member of the National Security Coun-

71

cil; he also prepares each year a comprehensive public statement on America's foreign policy. This takes the form of a report to Congress on the United States' up-to-the-minute position on preparedness and defense.

In such a position, with such responsibilities, it is little wonder that Secretary McNamara has been one of the most controversial figures in the Capitol's long history of men of controversy.

The basic charge most frequently hurled at Secretary McNamara is that he is a "human IBM machine" who disregards personal factors in his dealings with the American people. On the other hand, he has also been called a "brilliant administrator," and the "best Secretary of Defense we ever had."

So the question is often asked, "What is McNamara *really* like?" McNamara answers that question in these words: "I have always believed that if I had more facts than the other guy I would be ahead. I won't tolerate an emotional approach to any situation or problem."

McNamara has many detractors among the civilian as well as the military. He also has strong supporters, the strongest being his own boss, President Johnson. The President praised McNamara in the highest terms on an occasion when he presented Army Captain Roger H. C. Donlon with the Medal of Honor for heroism in Vietnam. In the midst of the elaborate White House ceremony, the President turned to his Secretary of Defense and said, "This man represents to me in our civilian life what Captain Donlon represents in the military life, the very best in America."

Robert McNamara was born in San Francisco on June 9, 1916, the eldest of two children. His sister's name is Margaret. He is of Irish-Scottish ancestry. His father, Robert James McNamara, was sales manager for a wholesale shoe company. His mother was the former Clara Nell Strange.

From childhood, McNamara was a rapid learner with a truly phenomenal memory. He was reading at the thirteen-year-old level when he entered the first grade. In high school at Piedmont, California, he earned a straight A record. He continued this brilliant record at the University of California at Berkeley, where he majored in economics and philosophy. At the end of his sophomore year he won the distinction of being elected to Phi Beta Kappa. He received his Bachelor of Arts degree in 1937.

During summer vacations, McNamara worked as a camp counselor and as an ordinary seaman. He made four trips to Hawaii, one to the Orient, and sailed through the Panama Canal.

McNamara continued his exceptional scholastic record at the Harvard University Graduate School of Business Administration. In 1939, he received his MBA —Master of Business Administration.

Following graduation from Harvard Business School, McNamara worked for one year with the accounting firm of Price Waterhouse & Company in San Francisco. In 1940 he returned to Harvard as an assistant professor. His students remember him as a hard and most exacting instructor.

When the United States entered World War II, McNamara volunteered but was rejected because of nearsightedness. He remained at Harvard, developing and conducting a special course for Army Air Force officers. At the same time he served the Air Force as a special consultant on establishing a statistical system to control the flow of personnel, materiel, and money. He took a leave of absence from Harvard in 1943 and went to England to establish statistical control systems for the Eighth Air Force. While on this job he was commissioned a captain.

During the remainder of the war, McNamara served with the Army Air Force in England, India, China, and the Pacific. He was awarded the Legion of Merit and had been promoted to lieutenant colonel by the end of the war. He now holds a colonel's commission in the Air Force Reserve.

It had been McNamara's intention to return to Harvard following his war service. Instead he was persuaded to join with nine other former Air Force statistical experts to form a group offering their specialized service to business corporations. The group was headed by Colonel Charles B. Thornton. They were hired by the Ford Motor Company in 1946. With the blessings of Henry Ford II, the group buzzed into every department, asking so many questions that they became known as the "Quiz Kids." Not for long though. The group's skillful analysis of problems and its sound recommendations for their solution soon earned it the more flattering epithet of "Whiz Kids."

McNamara's rise in the Ford Company was rapid. As manager of the company's planning and financial analyses offices, he gained the reputation of "knowing where every buck is spent," and, in 1949, was named controller of the company. By 1953 he had become assistant general manager of the Ford division. In this position he strongly urged the production of a Ford car that would appeal to the high-income as well as the low-income group, since America was in a period of rising prosperity. His advice was followed and Ford autos in two sizes quickly became top sellers in the motor industry. He became group vice-president of car divisions in 1957.

Other McNamara suggestions resulted in further success for the Ford Motor Company. He advised changing the Thunderbird from a two-seater to a four-seater, and Thunderbird sales tripled. He is also credited with the development of the Falcon, and was an early advocate of safety belts.

At the age of forty-four, McNamara was elected president of the Ford Motor Company on November 9, 1960, succeeding Henry Ford II. He was the first president of the company who was not a member of the Ford family.

At the time of his election to the presidency of Ford, the company was third largest in sales of all of America's industrial corporations.

Robert McNamara was president of Ford for just a few days over one month. The late John F. Kennedy had been elected President of the United States the same week that McNamara had been elected president of Ford. Kennedy scouts knew of McNamara, and his meteoric rise at Ford. They also knew that McNamara, although a registered Republican, had supported Kennedy in the Presidential race. That he had done so in the dominantly Republican circle of auto magnates was an impressive factor. McNamara and Kennedy had never met. Nevertheless, Kennedy asked McNamara to become his Secretary of Defense. The offer was accepted on December 13, 1960.

McNamara took the Cabinet post at considerable financial sacrifice. His annual salary as president of Ford has been estimated at no less than $100,000, and quite likely $500,000. He also gave up stock options of thirty thousand shares which would have meant profits of some $3,000,000 in his next three or four years as Ford president. McNamara gave all this up for a job which pays $25,000 a year. However, in the next few years, he will receive some $618,750 in deferred bonuses from Ford, earned in the years 1957 to 1960.

This explanation was given by McNamara for giving up a fortune to serve his country: "I had been approached about an assistant secretary's job under both the Truman and the Eisenhower administrations. At the time I felt I wasn't ready, financially or otherwise. I had once told Henry Ford that I was interested in public service. At some particular point I felt I would have to do it if I was asked. You just can't go on saying 'no' all your life."

The Secretary of Defense's feeling that public service should be the concern of all is deep-seated and goes back many years. While with Ford, he remained independent of the motor aristocracy that lives in lush Bloomfield Hills or Grosse Pointe, two of the most fashionable and exclusive suburbs of Detroit. Instead, he preferred a modest home in Ann Arbor, site of the University of Michigan.

In 1955, McNamara was asked to deliver the commencement address at the University of Alabama. He wrote his speech, and, as required, sent it to his superiors for clearance. They objected to one paragraph. It had to come out, they said. They felt that the paragraph inferred that young people should not consider entering the field of business based on the incentive of personal gain.

McNamara felt that the request was not a fair one, that his personal independence was being challenged, and that a matter of principle was at stake. On the day he was to deliver the speech, he drove alone out into the country. Standing beside his car, he read the speech aloud. An hour later, he was back on the campus and delivered his speech. The controversial paragraph remained in. It read:

"Today, progressive taxation places limits on the earning power of the businessman, and hence upon his purely monetary motivation. More and more he draws his incentive from a sense of public responsibility. More and more, I believe, idealistic and progressive young people will seek and find in industry not just a road to personal enrichment, but a most direct and effective means of public service."

McNamara's decision to give up one of the top jobs in the nation's industry was no surprise to his close friends. One of them said, "The shape of next year's bumper never did loom too large in Bob's life. He wants challenges."

He most certainly found them in the office of Secretary of Defense.

McNamara is the nation's eighth Secretary of Defense. The department was established in 1947, combining into one Cabinet office the former Cabinet posts of Secretary of War and Secretary of the Navy. It is a position that has been called "an impossible job," and a "man eater." *The New York Times* described the job as being one "to bring efficiency to a $40 billion enterprise beset by jealousies and political pressures while maintaining American military superiority." Since that description was written in 1960, the Defense Department's annual budget has risen to 50 billion dollars.

In supervising the operation of the largest department in the government, McNamara has made enemies among the military and in Congress. He is as aware of this as anyone, but criticism and opposition do not deter him if he thinks that he is right. An associate of McNamara's says of him, "When he feels something is right, you can't budge him. He's just got to do it."

Taking and holding such a firm position has led to the charge that the secretary runs the Defense Department as a "one-man" ruler, in addition to the charge that he is a "human IBM machine." By dominating the Joint Chiefs of Staff, and by consolidating the three branches of the nation's military—Army, Navy, and Air Force—under firm civilian control, he has made enemies in the Pentagon.

On Capitol Hill, he has been scorned by being termed "Robert (I've got all the answers) McNamara." He dazzles congressional committees with his statistics and percentages. Henry Ford once said of him, "He has the ability to keep in his head facts and figures that most people have to go to the records to get."

There is no doubt that McNamara is impressive and convincing as he spouts his endless statistics, and this very fact tends to annoy some members of Congress. Representative F. Edward Herbert, chairman of a subcommittee investigating McNamara's controversial Army reserve reorganization plan, summed up the feelings of many of his fellow members of Congress when he said, "Never in my twenty-five years have I seen such contempt for Congress as exhibited by Secretary of Defense

McNamara. He is a friend of mine. I like him. He's brilliant. He's the strongest Secretary of Defense we ever had—and therein lies the danger."

As to the charge that he is a "human IBM machine," one editor—a friend of McNamara's—wrote, "We think the Secretary of Defense ought, for a change, to take the same kind of cost-effectiveness look at humans that he does at hardware."

Even those who criticize the Defense Secretary admire his accomplishments, although grudgingly so. Almost all concede that he is the "strong man" of President Johnson's Cabinet. He has streamlined operations in the Pentagon. He has cut costs, at the same time building up America's military strength, and bringing more efficiency to its operations. He is, as another associate put it, "that man who provides the steel in the backbone of this [Pentagon] building."

If a box score were kept on McNamara's wins and losses in his many battles, he would come out ahead by a wide margin. He has at times battled head on with the armament industry, Congress, the Joint Chiefs of Staff, and the three branches of the nation's military. He has come off the winner every time.

McNamara is a dedicated man. He has given the same loyalty to President Johnson that he gave to the late President Kennedy. To McNamara, the job is the thing. He is determined to get it done, and he would give this same dedication to America's defense position under any President.

No one at the Pentagon works harder than the Secretary of Defense. His day begins at 7 A.M. when he arrives at the Pentagon and sits down behind his huge desk, once used by General John J. "Blackjack" Per-

shing of World War I fame. His day is crammed with
conferences, appearances before congressional committees, attendance at Cabinet meetings, studies of moun-
tainous reports, inspections of military installations all
over the world, and quick trips to Vietnam. Often,
McNamara is in his office long after the regular work-
day is over. Eight or nine o'clock at night finds him
alone at his desk, making notes on matters to be dealt
with the following day.

McNamara may well be the cold, efficient, machine-
like man he is described as when he is at work. At home
and with friends he is jolly, affable, and loves a good
conversational bout. Mountain climbing, skiing, and
camping are his favorite forms of relaxation. His wife is
the former Margaret Craig, a fellow student at the University of California. With his wife and three children
—Margaret Elizabeth, Kathleen, and Robert Craig—
McNamara can usually be found on the ski slopes at
Aspen, Colorado, during the height of the ski season.
On camping trips, he is the same early riser that he is at
work. He is first up, gets the fire going, and has the day
planned.

In appearance, McNamara is still quite youthful, although the lines in his face have deepened since he
moved into the Pentagon. He is lean, six feet tall, weighs
about one hundred and sixty-five pounds, dresses very
conservatively, and wears rimless glasses.

About his job as boss of the largest department in the
government, McNamara says: "I see my position as
being that of a leader, not a judge. I'm here to originate,
to stimulate new ideas and programs, not just to adjudi-
cate arguments. You've got to do things differently or
else you're not improving them."

By far the larger majority of observers of the Secretary of Defense agree that McNamara is doing exactly what he says in his description of his job. And his leadership is felt around the world.

LESTER BOWLES
PEARSON

THE CHIEF EXECUTIVE officer of Canada, Prime Minister Lester Bowles Pearson, has been described as a man who "is happiest when he's clinging to a precipice and just about to fall off."

For "Mike" Pearson—as his friends call him—political life has been one crisis after another. He thrives on crises, and, as he has proven again and again, he is at his best when confronted with problems which appear to be insurmountable.

Most world leaders reach that pinnacle after becoming leaders in their own countries. Lester Pearson reversed the process. He was an outstanding world figure long before he arrived at the top position in his own country, the Dominion of Canada.

In 1949, Pearson drafted the plan which resulted in

the North Atlantic Treaty Organization (NATO). He was president of the General Assembly of the United Nations in 1952–3. In 1956 it was his proposal for a United Nations international police force that put out the fire in the Suez Canal crisis when it threatened to blaze into a world war. For this he was awarded the Nobel Peace Prize in 1957.

Lester Pearson did not become prime minister of Canada until 1963. But before that he had a long record of service to his country. He became a civil servant in 1928 —thirty-five years before he became prime minister. Most of this service was in the external affairs of his country. Until the five or six years before he became Canada's top man, it could be said that he was better known in the councils of Europe and the United States than he was in his own country.

Lester Bowles Pearson was born on April 23, 1897, in Newtonbrook, Ontario, now a part of Greater Toronto. His parents were the Reverend Edwin Arthur and Annie Sara (Bowles) Pearson. He was the second of three sons. Reverend Pearson was an itinerant Methodist minister, moving about from town to town, and earning about seven hundred dollars a year. "We were rich," Pearson says, "in everything but money." It was a happy family, sternly religious, and highly interested in athletics. Pearson's father taught all his sons baseball, hockey, and football. Despite the shortage of money, all three Pearson boys were given good public school educations and went on to college.

Lester Pearson attended collegiate schools in Willowdale, Davisville, Aurora, Hamilton, and Peterborough. He entered Victoria College of the University of Toronto at the age of sixteen, in 1913.

World War I broke out when Pearson was in his second year at college. He joined the University's hospital unit and soon found himself in Salonika, Greece, attached to the British forces. An endless round of menial chores drove Pearson to transfer to the Canadian army and then to switch to the Royal Flying Corps. It was here that he was dubbed "Mike." His flight instructor thought Lester was a most inappropriate name for a fighter pilot. "From now on, you're Mike," he decided.

Mike never made it as a fighter pilot. After six weeks of training and only one and a half hours of actual flight instruction, he soloed. It was his first and last flight. He crashed coming into the landing strip when he tried to raise his plane over a high wire. The plane stalled and plummeted to the earth. Pearson was only shaken up and spent a week in the hospital.

On leave in London, Pearson was run over by a bus, and that put an end to his would-be career as a fighting man. He was invalided back to Toronto where, for the remainder of the war, he served as a flight instructor in Toronto.

In 1919, Pearson graduated from the University of Toronto with a Bachelor of Arts degree and honors in history. Then came a period when he stuffed sausages and hot dogs for Armour and Company in Hamilton, picking up extra money on the side by playing third base for the Guelph Maple Leafs, a semipro team. He was a good gloveman, but no hitter.

After a year of meat handling, Pearson applied for and received a scholarship to St. John's College of Oxford, and he was off to England. He distinguished himself at Oxford, scholastically and athletically. He received his degree in 1923 and was an outstanding hockey and lacrosse player. He was a member of Great Britain's Olympic hockey team at the 1922 Games.

Pearson's experience with Armour convinced him that he was not cut out for a business career. After finishing at Oxford, he was appointed as a history lecturer at the University of Toronto. Always a strong believer in physical fitness, he became part-time coach of the school's hockey and football teams. In one of his history classes, there was a very pretty student—Maryon Elspeth Moody, daughter of a Winnipeg doctor. They were married in 1925. "I taught her for one year," Pearson says with a grin, "and she's been teaching me ever since."

The turning point in Pearson's life came in 1928. By that time he was the father of a son, Geoffrey, and a daughter, Patricia, and was making a salary of eighteen hundred dollars a year. His future prospects were not bright, and he was feeling the same economic pinch that his father had felt before him. On a visit to Ottawa, capital of the Dominion, a friend of his, recently appointed chief of the new Department of External Affairs, suggested that Pearson enter government service. Pearson was reluctant. The friend persuaded him to take the examinations for the job of first secretary of the department. The tests were stiff. Pearson returned to Toronto, feeling that he had done nothing more than please an old friend. Much to his delighted amazement, he had passed with flying colors, getting the highest marks of all the candidates applying for the job.

From 1928 to 1935, Pearson served as the first secretary for the Department of External Affairs. He attended the Hague Conference on Codification of International Law, in 1930, and the London Naval Conference, in

1931. He also represented Canada at the London and Geneva disarmament conferences, and sat in on several sesssions of the League of Nations. He was building the firm diplomatic foundation which was to make him an outstanding international troubleshooter in the years to come.

In 1935, Pearson was posted to London as first secretary in the office of the High Commissioner for Canada and was soon promoted to secretary with the rank of counselor. In London he met leaders from all over the world. He took an intense dislike to do-nothing stuffed shirts. Pearson has never enjoyed the social or hoopla part of government and politics. He passed up the gay social life, the embassy cocktail parties, and dug deeply into the international situation. He returned to Ottawa in 1939, and informed Mackenzie King, then Canada's prime minister, that he felt certain an outbreak of war was imminent. King dismissed Pearson's warning, terming it ridiculous. Pearson cut his holiday short and returned to London. The war clouds had thickened during his short absence.

Pearson saw the horrors of the *blitz* of London by Nazi Germany's *Luftwaffe*. In 1941 he was called back to Ottawa to become Assistant Under Secretary of External Affairs. One year later found Pearson in Washington as minister-counselor of the Canadian Legation. When the legation was raised to embassy status, Pearson became Canada's ambassador to the United States.

Pearson's reputation as a skilled diplomat grew in Washington. He was well-liked, and easily won the confidence of Washington officials and emissaries of foreign governments. Many nights saw important world officials gathered around the piano in Pearson's Washington home, talking politics and singing.

During his first years in Washington, Pearson was an influential figure in the establishment of the United Nations Relief and Rehabilitation Administration (UNRRA). He was also named envoy extraordinary and minister plenipotentiary by Canada to the Dumbarton Oaks Conference, convened from August to October, 1944, to formulate preliminary plans for the United Nations. Following this exploratory conference, he represented his country as its senior adviser at the meeting in San Francisco of the United Nations conference on International Organization, and played an important part in drawing up the United Nations charter.

In 1946, Pearson was called back to Ottawa to become Secretary of State for External Affairs, succeeding Louis St. Laurent, who had become Canada's prime minister. In this important post, Pearson headed the Canadian delegation to the Japanese peace treaty conference, in 1951, and the London nine-power conference on German rearmament, in 1954.

As Secretary of State, Pearson advanced a suggestion that was to become a milepost in international relations. He drafted a speech for Prime Minister St. Laurent in which the formation of the North Atlantic Treaty Organization (NATO) was first proposed.

At the signing of this history-making treaty in Washington, on April 4, 1949, Pearson said: "This treaty, though born out of fear and frustration, must lead to positive social, economic, and political achievements if it is to live."

The treaty, an outstanding defensive bulwark for the Western powers, shot Pearson into the international spotlight. He remained there, serving as a member of the Canadian delegation to the United Nations General Assembly from 1946 to 1957. He was chairman of the delegation from 1948 to 1964, and served as president of the General Assembly's seventh session of 1952–3.

During these years, Pearson often served in the role of peacemaker in disputes among the United States, Great Britain, and Canada. He handled these situations skillfully and kept the relationships among the three nations running smoothly. However, Pearson was much more than a man who poured oil on troubled international waters. He never hesitated to criticize an action that he felt to be wrong. He demonstrated this in a speech that was highly critical of the United States when the United States asked the United Nations for a strong declaration that Communist China was the aggressor in the Korean conflict. The United Nations did pass such a declaration, but it was greatly watered down after Pearson's speech.

The Suez crisis found Pearson at the height of his diplomatic skill. Eventually, his suggestion brought about the solution of a most delicate situation that could have escalated into a third world war. Great Britain, France, and Israel invaded Egypt in October, 1956, over a dispute concerning the operations of the Suez Canal, the great waterway to the Far East. The United States opposed this move. Canada, always loyal to Great Britain, found itself forced to side with the United States against its mother country. The move by Great Britain, France, and Israel threatened to become a wedge between the United States and the Western powers.

Pearson moved quickly. He held a conference with John Foster Dulles, then Secretary of State of the United States. He talked with representatives of other United Nations' members. It was his proposal that the United Nations set up an emergency international police force to handle the Suez situation. This proposal was accepted by the UN by a 57–0 vote, with nineteen nations not voting. Two weeks later the first UN troops were on their way to Suez, and the crisis was over.

For this truly remarkable feat, Pearson was awarded the Nobel Peace Prize the following year.

The award was made to Pearson for "his powerful initiative, strength, and perseverance displayed in attempting to prevent or limit war operations and restore peace."

In 1957, only a few weeks after Pearson had received the Nobel Peace Prize, he was plunged to a low point. The Liberal Party, of which he became a member when he was part of the cabinet, lost power after having been in control for twenty-two years. John Diefenbaker succeeded St. Laurent as Canada's prime minister. Pearson became leader of the opposition.

In this position, Mike Pearson found himself clinging to precipices on several occasions. He made mistakes, mistakes which he publicly admitted but which cost the Liberal Party more seats in the Parliament. Diefenbaker called for an election, and the Conservative Party swept back into office with a clear majority of 208 seats to the Liberals' 49. The Liberal Party remained second until 1963. During those years, Pearson rebuilt the party. It was a difficult task, one that Pearson did because it had to be done, but not because he had any great relish for the tough game of politics.

Commenting on his feelings about rough and tumble politics, Pearson once said, "It has been said that I am not able to move people to tears of excitement. Quite probably that is true. The thing that terrifies me is demagoguery. The hoopla, the circus part of it, all that sort of thing still makes me blush."

But Pearson is always ready to come up with a cutting quip. During the 1963 campaign, he said of his opponent, Prime Minister Diefenbaker, "I would say to the Prime Minister, in the most kindly way possible, that he must not let failure go to his head." Diefenbaker had not made an impressive record as Canada's prime minister.

Pearson campaigned on the promise to "get Canada moving again, moving forward economically and back into the councils of the world." He called for a stepped-up program to get Canada rolling within sixty days of his taking office. This program was much more optimistic than it was realistic.

The Liberal Party won, but not by a clear majority. Of the 265 seats in the House of Commons, the Liberals won 129, the Conservatives 95, with the remaining 41 seats divided among minor parties. The Liberals were four seats short of the 133 seats needed for a clear majority. The Social Credit Party pledged its support to Pearson, and with these additional votes, the Liberals had the necessary majority, and Diefenbaker conceded defeat. Pearson became prime minister.

For the next two and a half years, Pearson served as Canada's chief executive but as head of a minority government. He wanted to change this. He wanted to be prime minister of a majority government. In 1965 he called for a national election. It was his hope to pick up four more seats for his Liberal Party, thus gaining a clear majority of the 265 seats in the House of Commons.

The election was held in November, 1965, and it solved nothing. The Liberal Party again captured 129 seats, still four short of a majority. If anything, Pearson lost some of his prestige at the hands of his old rival, Diefenbaker. The Conservatives picked up four seats.

Pearson continued as Canada's prime minister, operating as he had in the past. By again receiving support from the Social Credit Party, Pearson had a majority vote in the Commons on most of the legislation that he wanted to push through.

The possibility remained that Pearson would call another election, again seeking to gain a clear majority for the Liberals. But since Canada had had five elections in eight years, and elections are costly, it did not seem, early in 1966, that still another election would be called for some time. Canadians were sick of elections.

Pearson continued his efforts to get legislation through on three major points: national pension plans, old-age security, and medicare.

He is doing this while still clinging to a precipice. He may fail in his attempts to reach his goals, but he will have lived up to his own personal formula for life as he once publicly expressed it—"to deserve success rather than to achieve it."

WALTER
REUTHER

PROPHETICALLY, Walter (Philip) Reuther was born on the eve of Labor Day.

His first cry of protest was heard on September 1, 1907. Since that night, the voice of Walter Reuther has become louder, stronger, and more dominant, as he has risen from labor's rank and file to the leadership of a union numbering 1,500,000 workers.

Reuther is president of the United Automobile Workers (UAW). The formal name of the powerful organization is the International Union of United Automobile, Aircraft, and Agricultural Implement Workers, Congress of Industrial Organizations. Only Jimmy Hoffa's 1,750,000-member Teamsters' Union outnumbers the membership of the UAW.

In his rise to the stewardship of UAW, Reuther has faced violence and death several times. In the labor wars of the 1930's, thugs twice viciously beat him. In 1948 there was an attempt on his life. He was shot down in his kitchen, the blast of a shotgun almost tearing off his right arm. A year later, at Christmas, a package containing thirty-nine sticks of dynamite was delivered to Reuther's union headquarters.

To forestall further attempts on his life, Reuther, his wife, and two daughters moved into a house surrounded by a moat, behind a ten-foot fence, and the grounds are patrolled by German shepherd dogs and armed guards. Reuther never goes anywhere without one or more bodyguards.

No one was ever arrested for the attempts on Reuther's life. Police have so many places to look. Reuther is hated by the Communists, by the Ku-Klux Klan, by rival union leaders, and by "numbers" racketeers whom Reuther drove out of his unionized plants. When George Romney, governor of Michigan, was head of American Motors, he described Reuther as "the most dangerous man in Detroit." The shaggy-browed John L. Lewis, onetime president of the United Mine Workers and the CIO, called Reuther "a pseudo-intellectual nitwit." There are times, too, when even members of his own union look with some suspicion on their leader.

On the other side of the picture, however, Reuther has had Presidents of the United States among his supporters: Franklin D. Roosevelt, Harry S. Truman, Dwight D. Eisenhower, John F. Kennedy, and Lyndon B. Johnson. Praise for Reuther from the late Indian leader Jawaharlal Nehru came from far-off India; other

words of commendation by former Labor Party Minister Aneurin Bevan have come from Great Britain.

The New York Times labor writer A. H. Raskin,
writing in *The Atlantic*, stated: "The UAW is the most
zestful of America's big unions. Most of its qualities of
excitement have stemmed not from its strikes or even
its trailblazing exploits in collective bargaining, but from
the caliber of its officialdom."

Even within the hierarchy of motordom, Reuther has
his admirers. When Charles E. Wilson was president of
General Motors, he once said to Reuther: "I have great
respect for your ability and your leadership." This same
feeling was expressed by William S. Knudsen, General
Motors' prewar president. He and Wilson once suggested to Reuther that he leave labor's ranks and join
management. Reuther refused the offer.

Auto industry executives may admire Reuther, but
that does not mean that they like him. Asked the reason
for this, the answer is unanimous: "He's too effective."

Another reason for this dislike is the feeling that
Reuther goes too far. Industry leaders feel that he wants
to run both the union and the auto industry. This feeling flared openly when Reuther, right after World
War II, asked for a thirty per cent wage increase for
his union members, and at the same time stated that the
auto industry could grant this increase and still not raise
prices for new cars. Furthermore, he asked to examine
the auto companies' books, so that he could prove that
the manufacturers could grant his demands and still not
lose money.

Reuther's point was that if the thirty per cent wage
raise was passed on to the consumer, then the inflation-

ary spiral would cut into the raise since auto workers are car buyers themselves.

It is small wonder that motordom's executives blew up at this request. They said in no uncertain terms that Reuther was asking them to give up their rights to manage their own business. "Why don't you get back down to your own size?" one motor executive demanded of Reuther. "Do the job you're supposed to do—bargain for the money you want for your union members and give up your grand ideas of being a labor statesman."

Reuther did not win on this demand, but he did not give up either. Ten years later he proposed to Washington that a Public Review Board be established to watchdog the prices set by large corporations—all corporations, not just the motor industry. No such legislation has yet been proposed.

Fellow union leaders felt much as industry leaders about Reuther's idea. They said the union's job was to get money for its members, and it was management's right to decide whether the stockholders or the public paid for wage increases.

Whether one likes or dislikes, approves or disapproves of Walter Reuther, none can deny that he has fought for and won numerous gains for workers in the mass industries. These include increased monthly pensions, paid vacations, and regular yearly pay raises. One pay raise plan grants auto workers an automatic two and one-half per cent annual increase, allowing the worker his share in increasing productivity and sale of automobiles. Another wage increase plan is based on an escalator clause that raises workers' salaries when the cost of living rises.

These victories by Reuther for his union members were all firsts. Another equally important first won by the "Redhead"—as he is called—is what comes close to being a guaranteed annual raise. Auto companies agreed to supplement state unemployment insurance payments. This plan has spread to other industries, and unemployed workers receive up to sixty-five per cent of their regular pay for thirty-nine weeks, three fourths of a year.

These are the major gains that Reuther has won. There are others—a long list of fringe benefits including paid vacations, health plans, group insurance.

The smallest of the four Reuther brothers, Walter Philip Reuther was born in a two-family house in the mill section of Wheeling, West Virginia. His grandfather, a Social Democrat with a flowing beard, brought the Reuther family to America from his German farm in 1892. He objected to the compulsory Prussian military service in Germany and wanted to exempt his sons from it. His son Valentine, Walter's father, was a brewery truck driver and was deeply imbued by his father's socialistic beliefs. Valentine Reuther, while still in his early twenties, became the dynamic leader of the Brewery Workers Union. The four Reuther boys—Ted, Victor, Roy, and Walter—spent many Sunday afternoons listening to their father express his deep beliefs in justice and freedom.

Three of the brothers are now union members—Walter, Victor, and Roy. Ted became a chief clerk for Wheeling Steel, and his three brothers label him the "white sheep" of the family.

Walter Reuther quit Wheeling High School when he was fifteen to become an apprentice toolmaker, making

forty cents an hour. He was starting right at the bottom.
A member of the Wheeling YMCA, he once filled out
a questionnaire stating that he wanted to be either a
farmer or a labor leader. On the "Y" basketball team,
Walter was the center, even though his teammate,
brother Roy, was an inch taller. He was picked because
he was more spirited, hopping and twisting all over the
court.

Reuther maintains that same youthful bounce today.
He is almost always referred to as the youthful labor
leader and will probably go on being called youthful
when he is sixty, which will be in 1967. His thick shock
of red hair, his unlined face, and his trim, well-cared-for
body give him the perpetual look of the all-American
boy. He is five feet seven inches tall.

The job with Wheeling Steel lasted Reuther for three
years. He was fired for his attempt to organize fellow
workers against working on Sunday. He had heard that
there were plenty of jobs in Detroit, and off he went.
Soon he found out that he had been misinformed. Job-
less men were walking the streets of Detroit by the
thousands. The best job that Reuther could get was a
thirteen-hour night shift at the Briggs Motor plant. He
stuck this out for twenty-one straight nights—no days
off—then went over to Ford's Highland Park plant and
got a job as a toolmaker at $1.05 an hour. Five years
later he was one of Ford's highest paid mechanics and
the boss of forty men. His brothers Roy and Victor
joined him in Detroit.

Reuther finished his high school education at night
school, then enrolled at Wayne University with his
brother Victor. During his three years at Wayne, he
was active in the left-wing student movement, and an

ardent supporter of Norman Thomas when the Socialist leader ran for President in 1932. This activity cost him his foreman's job at Ford. It was the height of the Depression, and there were no jobs to be had. Victor was already unemployed. The two brothers put their heads together, added up their savings, and decided they had enough money for a trip to Europe.

The Reuther brothers went first to Germany where the tide of Nazism was rising. They saw the beginnings of Hitler's ruthless growing power. They left Germany, went to England, toured Belgium, France, and Italy on bicycles, then went to Russia. The brothers worked in a factory at Gorki for nearly two years. Reuther liked his fellow workers but developed an intense dislike for the Communist system, a feeling that remained with him in later days when he fought Communists in his own UAW.

Walter and Victor left Gorki, crossed over Asia, and arrived in Yokohama with exactly seven dollars between them. They were seven thousand miles from home. The American consul got them jobs on the steamship *President Hoover,* and they worked their way across the Pacific, spent their seaman's pay for bus tickets, and headed back to Detroit, with a brief stop-off to visit their family in Wheeling. The year was 1935 and Detroit seethed with wildcat strikes, lockouts, and blacklists.

Brother Roy was already engaged in union activity, and he was soon joined by Walter and Victor. In 1936, Walter took time out to marry the auburn-haired May Wolf, but on their wedding night the newlyweds traveled to another town where Reuther delivered a fiery organizing speech.

He got a job in General Motors' Ternstedt plant, devoting every free moment to union organizing, and became president of a new UAW union, Local 174. There were seventy-eight members of the local. As a result of this activity, he was fired and blacklisted. But Reuther was on the move. With the help of brother Victor, he lost no time in planning a sit-down strike at the Kelsey Hayes Wheel factory. The surprise strike caught management unprepared. Reuther agreed to call off the strike if management would permit him to sign up workers for his Local 174. Management conceded. Local 174's membership jumped from 174 to 2,400 members.

This increase was the first big upsurge in membership for the UAW. From then on, union membership shot skyward. Walter Reuther was a member of UAW's executive board, and the union's leading strike strategist. By 1937, the UAW boasted half a million members. Reuther, as director of the union's General Motors division, was the outstanding figure in the battle against the Big Three of motordom. General Motors was the first to recognize the UAW. Chrysler capitulated shortly after. Only Ford held out, Henry Ford announcing he would never recognize the UAW.

The Ford plant was filled with company spies. Henry Ford had hired a former prizefighter, Harry Bennett, who employed some three thousand thugs as a private army to fight the union organizers. In May, 1937, a group of union members—mostly women—headed by Reuther, started up the concrete overpass to a Ford plant to distribute leaflets. Bennett's thugs were lying in wait. They singled Reuther out. The "Battle of the Overpass" began.

Reuther testified as to what happened: "They [Bennett's men] picked me up eight different times and threw me down on my back on the concrete. While I was on the ground, they kicked me in the face, head, and other parts of my body . . . I never raised a hand. After they kicked me down all the stairs, they started to hit me at the bottom of the stairs, hit me, and slugged me, driving me before them, but never letting me get away."

The battle ended with Reuther lying bleeding on the trolley tracks in the street below the overpass. Women sobbed from being kicked in the stomach. One man's back was broken, another's skull fractured.

Ford reaped a harvest of bad publicity from the "Battle of the Overpass." When Reuther recovered, he returned to the overpass with hundreds of husky union men, and this time leaflets were distributed without molestation. But a year later, thugs invaded Reuther's Detroit apartment, and again he was severely beaten.

In 1941 the National Labor Relations Board ordered Ford to rehire some twenty-five-hundred workers who, the board found, had been illegally discharged, and to pay them two million dollars. A week later, Ford gave up the battle. He signed a contract with UAW—termed a "model" for the industry by UAW—and collective bargaining was finally won for the entire auto industry.

But the Redhead's battles were by no means over.

Communists were powerful in the UAW, and although Reuther twice pushed through anti-Communist resolutions at union conventions, the Reds struck back. They managed to get brother Victor defeated for high office in the state CIO. When, in 1940, Reuther called for aid to Britain, and pledged "no strike" by labor during the war years, the Communists struck again. Earl Browder, the Communist leader in America, took a full-page ad accusing Reuther of trying to wreck the auto industry.

Walter rode out these attacks and, as a vice-president of UAW, in charge of the union's General Motors division, he held his men in line during the war. There was much grumbling against the "no strike" pledge, and Reuther was even booed by his own members at UAW conventions.

In 1946, Reuther ran for the presidency of UAW against R. J. "Tommy" Thomas. Just before the vote, Reuther offered to shake hands with his rival. Thomas refused. Reuther smiled and said, "Tommy, if you're not big enough to lose, you're not big enough to win." Tommy lost. Reuther won by the narrow vote of 4,444 to 4,320.

But the Communists won two thirds of UAW's executive board, completely hamstringing the newly elected head of UAW. Reuther was able to hire his brother Victor as UAW's educational director, but that was just about the extent of his power. The executive board defeated him on several moves, and even passed out Communist-inspired literature and union statements without ever letting Reuther read them.

But the Redhead wasn't licked. As always, a tough fight brought out the best in him. He anticipated a Communist move to get rid of him entirely and met it with masterful skill. The Communist-dominated executive board's plan was to load the small Farm Implement Workers' union with five hundred extra delegate votes for the upcoming convention. Reuther's anti-Communist speakers worked fast. They exposed the phony move by the board, and when the election was over, the Communists found their strategy had backfired, and they were voted out. Reuther's forces captured eighteen of the twenty-two seats on the executive board. He lost no time in driving other Communists out of the UAW. Then he got rid of the numbers racketeers who were milking his members in their factory jobs.

Reuther was elected president of the Congress of Industrial Organizations (CIO) in 1952, after the death of Philip Murray. In 1955, the CIO and the American Federation of Labor (AFL) merged, to become the powerful labor organization called AFL–CIO. George Meany, who had been president of the AFL, became president of the newly joined unions. Reuther became one of the twenty-seven vice-presidents. Although he is not called the first vice-president, or assistant president, there is no doubt that he ranks right behind Meany as the number two man of the great labor organization. It is generally conceded by all labor authorities that there is little question that Reuther will become president of AFL–CIO on Meany's retirement or death.

As president of AFL–CIO, Reuther will be at the top of the strongest labor organization in the world. But his problems will by no means be ended. The most pressing one today is automation. The drop in union membership is evidence that automation has sharply cut down the number of workers in nearly every field. The UAW once had a membership of 1,500,000 workers. In 1965, the UAW's membership was down to 1,104,000 workers. And auto production was at its highest.

The Redhead has faced many problems in his long career. One more is not likely to stop him, even if it is one of the toughest he has yet to face. Reuther is always at his best when the going is toughest. The odds are that if anyone can handle the threat of automation to the nation's labor force, it will be Walter Reuther, the fighting Redhead.

WHEN A MAN consistently demonstrates an ability to win, he must be given thoughtful consideration for any goal he sets for himself. When his victories come against seemingly impossible odds, then he becomes somewhat of a phenomenon. Such a man is George Wilcken Romney, governor of Michigan.

Romney's two outstanding victories came in politics and in business. He was elected the Republican governor of a state in which the governor's chair had been occupied by Democrats for fourteen years. Furthermore, in Michigan the Democratic party is the majority party by a considerable margin.

Romney's first election to Michigan's highest office, in 1962, was by a margin of 78,000 votes. Running again in 1964, he increased that margin nearly five times, winning by 383,000 votes. He did this in a national election year which saw the Democratic Presidential candidate, Lyndon B. Johnson, carry the state by 1,100,000 votes over Republican Barry Goldwater. The Democrats also won every other state office, and for the first time in thirty years captured control of both houses of the legislature.

As a vote getter, Romney had definitely proven himself.

Romney's victory in the business world was equally sensational. In 1955, he became head of American Motors Corporation, a company near bankruptcy. It had lost $7,000,000 the year that Romney took over. Three years later, in 1958, American Motors Corporation showed an earned profit of $26,000,000.

When Romney became governor of Michigan, he was faced with another bankrupt situation. The state was broke—its treasury depleted. Two years later, the state treasury showed a whopping surplus of $105,000,-000.

As a moneymaker, Romney had definitely proven himself.

It is as a vote getter, though, that Romney continues to hold the headlines. After his victory in 1962, his name was prominently mentioned as the most likely Republican Presidential nominee in 1964. But the political pundits had failed to reckon with Barry Goldwater. When the 1964 Republican National Convention was over, Goldwater was the party's standard-bearer. Romney was mentioned briefly as a possible candidate, and he opposed Goldwater's nomination, but that was as far as he got.

After Goldwater's and the Republican party's defeat, and Romney's sensational victory, the name of Michigan's reelected governor again came to the fore as the most promising and most likely presidential Republican candidate for 1968. Romney had nothing to say on this subject during his second term as Michigan's governor.

There have been many other victories in Romney's life. He most certainly came up the hard way in the true "rags-to-riches" tradition. George Wilcken Romney was born on July 8, 1907, in a Mormon colony in Chihuahua, Mexico. The question of Romney's constitutional eligibility for the Presidency has been raised, since he was born in a foreign land. However, most experts on the Constitution believe that he *is* eligible because his parents were American citizens.

Romney's parents, Gaskell and Anna (Pratt) Romney, had moved to Mexico with other Mormon families ten years before George was born. When he was five, his parents and other members of the Mormon colony were driven out of the country by Pancho Villa, the Mexican rebel. The Romneys lived briefly in Texas, where the family was on government relief, before moving on to California, where Gaskell Romney tried the contracting business.

Although a hardworking man, Romney's father was plagued by financial reverses. He went broke five times, his most serious setbacks coming in the recessions of 1921 and 1929. He finally became a successful builder in Salt Lake City. Young George, one of six children, went to work when he was eleven. He grew up in Idaho and Utah, and among his boyhood jobs were picking sugar beets, peeling and canning tomatoes, and working as carpenter's helper. He became skilled as a lath and plaster workman.

Romney's elementary schooling was hit or miss, taken in whatever town or village the family happened to be living in. When he was fifteen, he entered the Latter-Day Saints School in Salt Lake City, working his way through the four-year course. Romney's advanced education consists of a brief period at the University of Utah and courses at George Washington University in Washington, D.C. He has no formal college degree.

On finishing at the Latter-Day Saints School, Romney spent a year working as a lather, and saved six hundred and thirty dollars. With this money he went to England for two years as a missionary for the Mormon Church. He received no compensation, since the church does not pay for such service. Romney's son Scott (the eldest of four children) also did overseas missionary work in the early 1960's.

During his two years in England, Romney developed his oratorical skill as an evangelist in Trafalgar Square and Hyde Park. He says he acquired there his talents for debating, quick thinking, and persuasion. These gifts have stood him in good stead both as a businessman and a politician.

After returning to the United States, Romney went to the West Coast to pursue his courtship of his high school sweetheart Lenore LaFount, who was having a brief career on the stage and in the movies. They were married and moved to Washington, D.C., where Romney entered the employ of Senator David I. Walsh of Massachusetts. This job was Romney's first brush with American politics. and it is said that his exposure was quite a shock to the deeply religious man who had been taught to believe that American politics were "divinely inspired."

After his stint with Senator Walsh, Romney turned to the world of business, and he was on his way up the ladder. The Romneys moved to Pittsburgh where he was employed by the Aluminum Company of America. From there he was transferred by Alcoa to Los Angeles as a salesman. In 1932, Romney returned to Washington and for the next six years was a lobbyist for Alcoa and the Aluminum Wares Association. For two years during this time, 1937 and 1938, he was president of the Washington Trade Association Executives.

During this period, Romney's work attracted the attention of Detroit's automobile manufacturers. In 1939 the Romney family moved to Detroit where he became Detroit manager and later general manager of the Automobile Manufacturers Association. As a director of the association, he was the automobile makers' chief spokesman during World War II and an industry adviser on war production and personnel.

Romney joined the Nash-Kelvinator Corporation, and when it merged with American Motors he became president and chairman of the board of directors. His decision to make a car that the "Big Three"—General Motors, Chrysler, and Ford—did not have was to change American motor habits in the years to come. He decided to manufacture a small, compact car to compete with the "gas-guzzling dinosaurs"—his phrase—turned out by the Big Three. The result was the compact Rambler, which pulled American Motors out of the red into the black and started the vogue for the compact car in the United States. The Big Three soon followed with their own compacts.

The magazine *Business Week,* commenting on Romney's success with his Rambler, said: "To auto industry observers, too often tempted to believe that General Motors, Ford, and Chrysler have a monopoly on brains, George Romney looks like the smartest or luckiest man in Detroit."

There was much more "smart" than "luck" in Romney's intense drive to lift American Motors out of the red and raise it to a highly profitable organization. He approached the task with the zeal of a crusader and the confidence of a supersalesman. He hopped all around the country, in and out of salesrooms, in and out of Ramblers, demonstrating them, praising them, selling them. He prepared himself well for this job, a characteristic of Romney's for any goal he sets for himself. As a vice-president of American Motors he learned his product inside out. He attended night classes at the company's service school. He worked on the assembly line. When he reached a point where he could take a Rambler apart and put it back together again, he was ready to sell the car to America. And he did.

He hammered the phrase "gas-guzzling dinosaurs" into motorists' minds. He had scale-model dinosaurs built and used them in his inspirational sales speeches. To demonstrate how a small item could carry as much punch as a large one, he placed a vitamin pill alongside a loaf of bread. Disheartened American motor salesmen and dealers had their spirits raised by Romney's favorite song, "Stouthearted Men," which became the company's unofficial anthem.

Romney brought his own personal, contagious excitement to the selling of motor cars. His basic idea that the American car buyer in large numbers might well want a small compact, more economical than those being produced by the Big Three, paid off.

Pulling American Motors out of its economic hole was a job that would occupy the full time of the most resourceful and energetic of executives. But for the restless, driving Romney there was more to be done. He felt he had an obligation to his community. He organized and became chairman of a group to study conditions in Detroit's public schools—the schools themselves were in a position similar to that of the pre-Romney American Motors Corporation. Even this extra task was not enough. His successful "citizen's approach" to Detroit's school problems was now adapted to the state's fiscal problems. The state of Michigan was in a financial bog, resulting from the long conflict between the Democratic Governor G. Mennen Williams and the Republican-controlled legislature. A nonpartisan Citizens for Michigan group was formed, with Romney at its head. The group decided that the best way to repair Michigan's state government was to revise its constitution. This idea was not new. It had been suggested as far back as 1908, but nothing had ever been done about the overhaul. Citizens for Michigan and Romney did do something about it. They won public approval for a constitutional convention in 1961.

It was about this time that Romney's name began cropping up for political office. It was thought that he might seek the governorship. But he emphatically withdrew his name from any consideration.

Early in 1962—February—he did announce his candidacy, and his announcement made sensational headlines. It was reported that before making his decision to run, Romney had prayed and fasted for twenty-four hours. This story was true. Romney himself said, "It is the regular practice of people of my faith to fast and pray before an important decision."

But the fast was played up big in the newspapers and used as highly charged ammunition by his political enemies. Romney was deeply hurt and angered by the reaction to his fasting. "It was a private and personal thing," he stated.

Mrs. Romney, in an article in *Good Housekeeping* magazine, had this comment on the much-publicized fasting: "Our family believes with all our hearts in the teachings of our Church, and we always try to practice our faith. Fasting is basic to our worship. And prayer on appropriate occasions is to us like breathing. I think there are times in everyone's life when he or she feels the need for guidance beyond that of man."

At this time Romney was president of the Detroit Stake of Our Church of Jesus Christ of Latter-Day Saints. The position is comparable to that of a bishopric. The *Town Journal* describes Romney's duties in his church position this way: "He supervises the religious work of some twenty-seven-hundred members in his district, preaching occasional sermons, and takes his turn at manual labor in projects which the church undertakes."

Of his religion, Romney says, "My religion is my most precious possession. Except for it, I could easily have become excessively occupied with industry. Sharing responsibility for church work has been a vital counterbalance in my life."

Since becoming governor of Michigan, Romney has resigned as president of the Detroit Stake.

The greatest controversy about Romney's political future stems from his Mormonism. It is said that his political philosophy is based on the Mormon religion. "He is a deeply religious man," a friend has said, "who has a great belief in the individual and the family. For him, each person is a distinct personality and child of God." As for the American political system, it is Romney's sincere belief that it is "divinely inspired," and will one day spread over the globe to relieve all peoples from bondage.

When Romney first got his feet wet politically, he shied away from political labels, even to the extent of avoiding the Republican label under which he was running for governor.

"We need an approach free from narrow partisanship," he said, and was equally critical of the Republican party's business influence and the Democratic party's labor influence.

His campaign for governor was conducted at the same feverish pace that he had used in putting over the Rambler. His nonpartisan appeal pulled many Democratic votes to his side—votes he had to get in Michigan —and he won handily over his Democratic opponent.

Romney, although a Republican governor who attends Republican governor's conferences and tries to heal the split in the Republican party, still does not like hard-and-fast labels. He feels that partisanship is wrong. "This is the side of politics I think is crazy," he states. "As far as I'm concerned, you ought to be for things because they are right and not because of party labels."

This strong belief on Governor Romney's part comes through when he states how he makes up his mind about an issue. "Once you have searched out the facts and have prayed and reached a point where you think you have an answer to the question you are undertaking to solve, then the third step is to be believing. That means to believe that the decision you have made is the right one, and to put everything you've got into carrying it out."

George Romney is a handsome man. He stands five feet, eleven inches tall, weighs around one hundred and seventy-five pounds, and maintains an athletic figure. He believes in physical fitness. One of the Mormon precepts is a fit body, since the body is the "temple of the spirit." Romney plays golf every morning of the year, except when snow lies deep on the golf course. He gets in eighteen holes by using three balls to play six holes, literally running between each shot. He neither smokes nor drinks liquor or stimulants, not even tea or coffee.

Romney may well have set his sights for the Republican Presidential nomination in 1968. But he has made no public announcement to this effect. During his second term as governor, he became much more of a Republican-party team man than he had ever been before. He named Mrs. Elly M. Peterson chairman of the Michigan state party. Mrs. Peterson was formerly Assistant Republican National Chairman and is well connected with Republican party leaders throughout the country. Romney himself has widened his area for speaking, appearing at functions all over the United States.

Many political professionals in the Republican party do not like Romney. "Romney won't swallow everything out of party loyalty," one pro says of him. "That's why some party pros around the country don't like him."

If Romney seeks and gets the Republican Presidential nomination in 1968, just what chance would he have against President Lyndon B. Johnson, assuming the President runs for reelection? That is a question asked by many, and the replies are almost universal that the odds would be high against him. They would be high against any man the Republicans put up. That is another reason why, among the pros in the Republican party, they might be quite willing to "let George do it."

The odds have been high against Romney before.

INDEX